Home Made

200 Creative Concoctions and Practical

Potions for Crafts, Beauty Aids, Household Products,

and Gifts from Your Kitchen

Home Made

200 Creative Concoctions and Practical Potions for Crafts, Beauty Aids, Household Products, and Gifts from Your Kitchen

Alexa Lett

A Perigee Book

A Perigee Book
Published by The Berkley Publishing Group
A division of Penguin Putnam Inc.
375 Hudson Street
New York, New York 10014

Copyright © 2001 by Alexa Lett
Text design by Tiffany Kukec
Illustrations by Lynn Jeffrey
Cover design by Jill Boltin
First edition: May 2001

Published simultaneously in Canada.

The Penguin Putnam Inc. World Wide Web site address is
www.penguinputnam.com

Library of Congress Cataloging-in-Publication Data

Lett, Alexa.
Home made : 200 creative concoctions and practical potions for crafts, beauty aids,
household products, and gifts from your kitchen / Alexa Lett.
p. cm.
Includes index.
ISBN 0-399-52697-8
1. Handicraft. I. Title.

TT157 .L427 2001

745.5—dc21   00-051049

Printed in the United States of America

10 9 8 7 6 5 4

NOTICE: The recipes contained in this book are to be followed exactly as written. Neither the publisher nor the author is responsible for your specific health or allergy needs that may require medical supervision, or for any adverse reactions to the recipes contained in this book.

To my sweet friend Sadie,

the one who calls me Mom. May we always

create good things together.

Contents

Preface

Please use this book as a guide to create wonderful and unusual projects. My experience as a skilled chef is nonexistent. My experience as a "trial and error" creator of fun and goofy projects is great!

The appliances in my home serve as tools to further expand my creations and experiments. They have a secondary purpose of providing somewhat nutritional sustenance for my family.

Use this book with the greatest of cooking intentions. Read, create, cook, blend, stir and call for takeout. Keep in mind that nothing you will make from these recipes will be edible!

Tools and Definitions of the Trade

Clean cans: Most any type of thoroughly cleaned food can is useable—soup, vegetable, coffee, etc. Make sure there are no sharp edges left after opening.

Containers: Think creative recycling. You don't have to buy containers to make molds for the projects in this book. You can use old flowerpots, odd glasses, creamers, sugar bowls or saltshakers.

Double boiler: One of the most often called for tools in the book is the double boiler. But I recommend that you do not use the same pots and pans for these projects that you use for cooking because many recipe ingredients will leave a residue. For an inexpensive double boiler, simply use a clean, 16-ounce can (about the size of a standard coffee can) with a medium-sized saucepan.

Food processor: Any size machine will work for many fine grinds and processing. For the most part, ingredients in this book that require processing will not damage or leave residue on the container of the machine.

Grater: Any kind of grater with large holes will work. The stand-up four-sided variety is the most versatile.

Lidded jars and bottles: Always wash, clean and dry any recycled glass containers before use. Virtually any type of glass jar can be used for the projects in this book, but make an effort to collect lots of smaller types such as baby food, jam samplers (like the kind you get in hotels) or even old perfume bottles. Plastic containers may not always be best for storing.

Microwave oven: As there are variations in microwave ovens depending on the size and other factors, you may have to adjust the heating times and temperature to your own model.

Molds: Use any container that can be used to give shape to soap, candles or other items that start in a liquid form. Try individual disposable yogurt or applesauce cups, small margarine tubs, commercially available plastic candy molds, small drawer organizer cups, tart tins and hollow plastic toys.

Many of the soap recipes call for a 5-ounce mold. But this is a general guideline only because an ounce is a weight measure rather than a volume measure. Tip: Spray the mold with oil before use to allow the item to slide out easily. Avoid containers with deep ridges.

Pots and pans: It is always best when crafting to use pots and pans specifically dedicated to that use. Often, ingredients in the recipes will leave a residue that might be harmful or alter the taste of food.

Squeeze and pump bottles: Recycle one of the many food or personal care product containers such as ketchup, mustard, lotion or hairspray. Always wash, clean and dry any recycled bottles before use.

The Well-Stocked Creative Pantry

Alum: A form of sulfate most commonly used in pickling; available in grocery stores

Ammonia: A pungent, colorless, gaseous alkaline often used for cleaning and disinfecting; available in grocery and hardware stores

Baking soda

Beeswax: A solid form of wax in mesh sheets; available in craft or candle-supply stores

Birthday candles: Small 3- to 4-inch candles available in packs of 8 or more; available in the baking section of the grocery store in party and stationery stores

Camphor oil: A medicinal oil; available in drugstores

Candles: Save all the old ends of your candles to recycle into new shapes and sizes

Castile soap: A brand-name all-natural, unscented bar soap; available in grocery and drugstores

Chlorine bleach

Club soda

Cooking oil: Any vegetable oil. Generally, you will not want to use any animal fats in the projects in this book

Corn meal: Any brand corn meal; white or yellow

Cornstarch

Cotton balls

Crayons: Use all those odd bits of broken crayons lost under the sofa

Epsom salt: A brand of medicinal salt available in drug and grocery stores

Essential oil: Concentrated perfume oils; available in health-food, vitamin and craft stores

Flour: For most projects, you will use white flour

Flowers: The recipes listed in this book require certain varieties of fresh or dried flowers chosen primarily for their aromatic qualities.

Food coloring: Liquid, paste and powder coloring; available in grocery and baking stores

Fragrance oil: Diluted essential oil

Gelatin, unflavored: A powdered form of gelatin used to thicken mixtures; available in grocery stores

Glycerin: An all-natural, unscented soap that has a slight yellowish color; available in a solid and liquid form in health-food, vitamin and drug stores

Ivory Snow: The name-brand all-natural, unscented washing powder

Kitty litter

Liquid starch

Mineral water: The same bottled water used for drinking

Orrisroot: A fragrant rootstock made from the root of the iris; generally available in powdered form in grocery stores

Pinecones

Plaster of paris: A type of powdered compound used for casting, available in craft and hardware stores

Poster paint: A water-based paint; available in craft and school-supply stores

Powdered paint pigment: A concentrated paint powder; available in craft and school-supply stores

Rock salt: This is the kind of large crystal salt used in ice-cream makers

Salt: Unless otherwise specified, the recipes call for standard table salt

Sand: Typical beach sand purchased for the sandbox; available in hardware stores or building or garden centers (Sand collected from the local beach may have lots of undesirable stuff in it, so it's best to buy it.)

School glue

Shellac: A clear protective spray; available in craft and hardware stores

Sugar: Those recipes that call for sugar use white

Talcum powder

Tempera paint powder: A powder form of nonoil-based paint; available in art and school-supply stores

Treated castor oil: A medicinal liquid; available in drugstores

Turpentine: A liquid paint thinner; available in hardware stores

Vinegar: The recipes generally call for white or cider vinegar; available in grocery stores

Witch hazel: An astringent alcohol solution; available in drugstores

CHAPTER ONE

Face-It
Look-Good Recipes

Creative Concoctions for

Facials, Masks,

Steams and Scrubs

Breakfast Facial

Eggs have so many uses—edible and not. The egg whites act as a wonderful tightening agent for the skin.

The whites of two eggs

In a small bowl, whip the whites of the two eggs with an electric blender until they are frothy and have peaks.

Spread the egg whites over your face (not too close around the eyes). Lie down and think good thoughts until it dries completely. Rinse well with warm water.

Citri-Meal Facial Scrub

MAKES ENOUGH FOR THREE TREATMENTS.

2 tablespoons fine oatmeal

1 tablespoon dried ground orange peel

Grind the oatmeal and orange peel together in a food processor. You want it to be as fine a powder as possible. Keep in a lidded jar in the bathroom.

In the palm of your hand, mix 1 teaspoon of the mixture with just enough warm water to create a paste. Rub the paste gently into your skin, then rinse with warm water.

Facial Rinse

I pint white vinegar

2 cups chopped petals or leaves (sage, yarrow or lemon balm)

In a saucepan, bring the vinegar to a boil and add the chopped petals/leaves. Remove from heat, cool and transfer to a large covered container. Let steep for 2 weeks. Strain through a coffee filter. Discard solids and store liquid in a covered glass jar. This rinse will last several weeks.

Use 2 tablespoons of mixture to every 1/2 gallon of water. Splash on face several times.

Facial Steam

If you would like your face to feel refreshed,
try this invigorating facial steam.

4 tablespoons dried peppermint or lavender leaves

5 cups water

In a large saucepan, bring the herbs and water to a boil. Pour the mixture into a large heat-proof bowl. Drape a large towel over your head and shoulders so it envelops the bowl, forming a tent. Keep your face about a foot away from the surface of the water. (This is not recommended for those who suffer from breathing or heart problems.) After steaming your face for 5 to 10 minutes (lift the towel to get a cool breath as needed) rinse your face with a cool, damp cloth. Yum!

Herbal Tea Mask

1 cup herbal tea (peppermint or chamomile)

Brew the herbal tea. Let cool slightly. Totally saturate a soft cotton cloth in the warm tea. Squeeze out the excess tea, and cover your face with the warm cloth. Lie down for about 10 minutes until the cloth is cool. Rinse your face with warm water and moisturize.

Honey Meal Mask

1 cup water

1/2 cup dried chamomile

2 tablespoons honey

2 tablespoons oatmeal

Heat the water and chamomile in a small saucepan. Remove from heat, and stir in the honey and oatmeal. Let the mixture cool to room temperature.

Apply to your face in an upward circular motion. Let the mask remain on your face for about 30 minutes. Peel off and rinse with warm water.

Jelly Facial Mask

2 ounces glycerin

3/8 ounces dry pectin

2 ounces herbal tea

Stirring the glycerin, gradually add the dry pectin until combined. Add the herbal tea and mix thoroughly. Refrigerate overnight to thicken. It will keep in the refrigerator for about a week in a covered container.

Apply to your face and neck, and let it stay on for about 10 minutes. Rinse with warm water and moisturize the skin.

Kitchen Facial Mask

Remember the good ol' days when you could make anything in your kitchen? Well, this facial mask literally comes from the bygone years. Our grandparents used to use Fuller's Earth on their skin to absorb all the toxins.

¹/₂ cup plain yogurt

¹/₂ teaspoon Fuller's Earth (available at drugstores)

1 teaspoon honey

3 drops chamomile oil

Blend all the ingredients thoroughly.

Apply to your face and neck. Leave on your skin for 10 to 12 minutes. Rinse with warm water and moisturize your skin using Creamy Rose Cream on page 28.

CHAPTER TWO

Soaps to Whet the Appetite

Soothe and

Clean Naturally

Candy Mold Soap

This is great cleaning treat for the kids. They can make their own soaps and, one hopes, enjoy taking a bath more often.

1³/₄ cups Ivory Snow powder

¹/₄ cup water

Food coloring

Mix the soap powder and water together in a large bowl, adding the water a few drops at a time at the end until you get a thick consistency. If you want more than one color, divide the mixture into separate bowls. Add the food coloring, and stir until color is blended. Pour the mixture into plastic candy molds and allow to harden. This could take a few days or up to a week, depending on the size of the molds. To test for hardness, press lightly in the middle of the soap mold. It will gradually harden to the point you cannot make an indention with your finger. When the soaps feel hard to the touch, take them out of the molds and let them dry a couple more days.

Chamo-Mint Soap

This soap makes you feel extra clean,
because of the pleasing fresh fragrance.

4-ounce bar Castile soap

1/4 cup distilled water

2 tablespoons dried chamomile

1 drop red food coloring

1 tablespoon liquid lanolin

1 teaspoon jojoba oil

10 drops peppermint oil

4 drops vitamin E oil (squeezed from a vitamin E capsule)

Shred the Castile soap with a grater and set aside. Bring the water to a boil in a small saucepan and add the chamomile. Remove from heat, cover and let this steep for 30 minutes. Strain the chamomile from the water, return the water to the pan and reheat over low. Add the food coloring and shredded soap stirring continuously until it becomes sticky. Add the lanolin, jojoba oil, peppermint oil and vitamin E oil and blend. Remove the soap from heat and spoon into a 5-ounce mold. Let harden for several hours.

Cinnamon Soap

There is nothing like the heady smell of cinnamon to conjure visions of the winter holidays.

4-ounce bar unscented glycerin soap

15 drops cinnamon oil

1 drop red food coloring

In a double boiler, melt the glycerin soap over low heat until liquefied. Remove the pan from heat and stir in the cinnamon oil and food coloring. Pour the soap in a 5-ounce mold and let harden for several hours.

Fizzy Tomato Soap

*Sometimes soap could do with a little sizzle or perhaps
a unique fragrance. This soap has both.*

4-ounce bar unscented glycerin soap

5 tablespoons tomato juice

1/2 teaspoon red wine vinegar

10 drops lemon oil

1 teaspoon baking soda

In a double boiler, melt the glycerin soap until liquefied.
Stir in the tomato juice, red wine vinegar and lemon oil.
Remove the pan from heat and stir in the baking soda
until dissolved. Pour the soap in a 5-ounce mold
and let harden for several hours.

Green Thumb Soap

Gardeners will love this soap. It has texture to scrub away grime and dirt, yet it's soft and gentle for your hands.

4-ounce bar Castile soap

2/3 cup distilled water

2 tablespoons dried lavender

2 tablespoons dried rosemary

3 tablespoons yellow cornmeal

1 teaspoon liquid lanolin

5 drops essential oil scent of your choice

Shred the soap with a greater and set aside. In a small saucepan, bring the water to a boil. Add the herbs, and remove the pan from heat. Cover and let herbs steep for 30 minutes. Strain the herbs and return the liquid to the pan. Over low heat, reheat the water, then stir in the shredded soap. Stir until the mixture gets sticky to the touch. Remove the pan from heat and add the cornmeal, lanolin and essential oil. Stir. Spoon the mixture into a 5-ounce mold and let harden for several hours.

Java Cream Soap

This soap smells so good you'll want to drink it! Packaged with a bag of designer coffee, it makes the perfect gift for any coffee lover.

4-ounce bar unscented glycerin soap

2 teaspoons ground coffee beans

I teaspoon heavy whipping cream

I teaspoon aloe vera gel

Melt the glycerin soap in a double boiler over low heat. Add the ground coffee, whipping cream and aloe vera. Stir. Pour the mixture into a 5-ounce mold and let harden for several hours.

Lavender Soap Balls

2 (4-ounce) bars of Castile soap

1/3 cup water

1 tablespoon dried lavender buds

4 drops lavender oil

Food coloring (optional)

Shred the two bars of Castile soap with a grater and set aside. In a small saucepan, boil the water. Remove from heat, and add the lavender buds. Cover and steep for 15 minutes. Reheat the water and lavender mixture, and add the lavender oil. Slowly pour in the shredded soap. Let cool. For a particular color, add a couple drops of food coloring and blend. With your hands, knead the soap and form into balls. Let the soap balls dry on waxed paper for 2 to 5 days.

Lemon Peel Soap Bar

This soap has the clean smell of freshly squeezed lemons.

1 bar Ivory soap

1/3 cup water

1 1/2 tablespoons dried lemon peel

8 drops lemon fragrance oil

3 drops lemon juice

Shred the soap and set aside. In a small saucepan, bring the water to a boil. Remove from heat and add the lemon peel and let simmer for 4 to 5 minutes. Add the lemon fragrance oil, then slowly add the soap and stir until well blended. Sir in the lemon juice. Spoon the mixture into a 5-ounce mold and let harden for several hours.

Loofah Soap

This soap is filled with texture. The bits of loofah sponge exfoliate the skin. It is also great to scrub exceptionally dirty hands and feet.

I square inch dried loofah sponge

4-ounce bar of Castile soap

I teaspoon liquid lanolin

I teaspoon aloe vera gel

15 drops lemon oil

I drop yellow food coloring

Shred the loofah sponge into tiny pieces (a coffee grinder or mini food processor works well) and set aside. In a double boiler, melt the soap slowly over medium-low heat. Remove the pan from the heat and add the lanolin, aloe vera gel, lemon oil and food coloring. Stir. Add the loofah shreds and stir. Pour the mixture into a 5-ounce mold and let harden for several hours.

Oatmeal Soap

Our grandparents used to make this kind of soap.

4-ounce bar Castile soap

1/4 cup regular dried oats

1/4 cup distilled water

1 tablespoon dried chamomile

1 tablespoon dried rosemary

1 tablespoon jojoba oil

Shred the soap and set aside. Grind the oats in a food processor or coffee grinder and set aside. In a pan, bring the water to a boil. Add the chamomile and rosemary and let steep in pan for 30 minutes. Strain the herbs and return the water to low heat. Add the soap, stirring continuously until mixture is sticky to the touch. Remove the pan from heat and stir in the oats and jojoba oil. Spoon the soap into a 5-ounce mold and let stand for 6 to 8 hours.

Oatmeal Soap-on-a-Rope

This soap is environmentally positive because it uses
bits and pieces of leftover soap; it's fun and easy to make and it's
quite useful in the shower.

¹/₂ **cup oatmeal**

¹/₂ **cup soap crumbs (broken small pieces or hotel bar-sized soap)**

1 ¹/₂ **tablespoon vegetable oil**

1 ¹/₂ **tablespoon water**

16-**inch piece of cotton rope or cord with a knot tied at one end**

Blend the oatmeal and soap crumbs in a blender. Use the pulse option until the mixture becomes quite fine. Put the oatmeal and soap mixture in a large, deep mixing bowl. Add the oil and water and mix well. Using your hands, form the mixture into a ball. Divide the ball into two equal parts with a knife. With your finger, make a small indention on the cut sides, and place the rope in the middle of the split ball. Gently mold the two halves back together. The rope or cord should be hidden within the ball, all except for the knot and about 12 inches of cord. Let the soap dry for about 3 days, in the sunshine if possible.

Orange Creamsicle Soap

This soap reminds me of the frozen treats I used to buy
off the ice-cream truck in my neighborhood!
Yummy!

4-ounce bar of unscented glycerin soap

5 drops orange oil

1 drop orange food coloring

2 tablespoons heavy whipping cream

5 drops vanilla fragrance oil

In a double boiler, melt the soap over low heat. Remove from heat. Stir in orange oil, food coloring, whipping cream and vanilla fragrance oil, one at a time. Pour into a 5-ounce mold and let harden for several hours.

Peachy Cream Soap

4-ounce bar Castile soap

1/4 cup distilled water

1/4 cup powdered milk

1 tablespoon sweet almond oil

1/4 teaspoon peach fragrance oil

1 drop orange food coloring

Shred the Castile soap and set aside. Heat the water in a saucepan over low heat. Slowly stir in the soap until it is sticky to the touch. Remove the pan from heat and stir in the powdered milk, almond oil, peach fragrance oil and food coloring until blended. Spoon the mixture into a 5-ounce mold and let harden for several hours.

Simple Scented Soap

This is one-of-a-kind gift to give a friend who really likes a particular scent but for which no commercially produced soap is available. Your friend will know you were thinking of her.

1 (4 by 16-inch) piece of muslin fabric

Favorite perfume/cologne

1 bar of unscented soap such as Castile or Ivory

Heavily spritz the muslin with the perfume/cologne. Wrap the fabric as many times as possible around the bar of soap. Drop it in a plastic resealable bag, seal it and leave for 2 months. You will be surprised how long the soap will hold the scent.

Vanilla Almond Soap

4-ounce bar Castile soap

1/4 cup distilled water

1 tablespoon sweet almond oil

1 teaspoon vanilla fragrance oil

1/2 cup shredded almonds

Shred the Castile soap and set aside. Heat the water in a pan over low heat. Slowly stir in the soap until it is sticky to the touch. Remove the pan from the heat and add the sweet almond oil, peach fragrance oil and shredded almonds. Blend. Spoon the mixture into a 5-ounce mold and let harden for several hours.

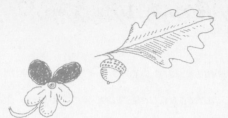

CHAPTER THREE

Personal Pampering Recipes

Indulge Yourself with

Beautiful Creams, Bath Oils,

Bubble Bath and More

Creamy Rose Cream

This moisturizer makes a superior face cream. Get into your most comfortable flannel jammies, lather up and relax with a good black-and-white movie on television.

1/2 cup rose water

1/2 teaspoon glycerin

2 tablespoons witch hazel

1/4 teaspoon borax

2 tablespoons white beeswax

1 teaspoon liquid lanolin

3 tablespoons almond oil

5 drops rose oil

In a saucepan over medium-low heat, heat the rose water, glycerin, witch hazel and borax until the borax has dissolved. In a double boiler, melt the beeswax, lanolin and almond oil over low heat. Slowly add the rose water mixture to the beeswax mixture. It will begin to turn milky and thicken. Turn off the heat and continue to stir as it cools, about 5 to 10 minutes. Add the rose oil a drop at a time and continue to mix. Once thickened, pour the cream into lidded glass jars. This cream will keep for several months.

Cucumber Cream

After a hard day in the sun, cool your skin with this refreshing cream. Simply apply to your face or body, let dry for 5 minutes and rinse with warm water.

1 whole cucumber, unpeeled

¹/₂ ounce white paraffin

2 ounces sweet almond oil

Cut the cucumber in chunks and puree it in a food processor. Strain the pulp through a colander lined with cheesecloth. Place the wax in a medium microwave-safe container, cover loosely with waxed paper or plastic wrap and melt the wax in the microwave on medium for 90 seconds. Remove the wax from the oven and slowly stir in the sweet almond oil. Add strained cucumber and mix thoroughly. Let the mixture cool completely, then store in a lidded glass container in the refrigerator. The cream should keep for 60 days.

White Glove Hand Cream

This is a good remedy for dry or chapped hands because it works all through the night. Before you go to bed, generously cover your hands with the cream and slip on a pair of cotton gloves. Wake up the next morning with soft, supple hands. This cream also makes a wonderful hostess gift along with a fine pair of white cotton gloves.

1 bar unscented hard white soap

6 tablespoons boiling water

4 ounces beeswax

4 tablespoons glycerin

2/3 cup almond oil

4 tablespoons rose water

20 drops patchouli oil

Grate the soap and place it in a heat-resistant bowl. Add the boiling water and stir until the mixture is dissolved and smooth. In a double boiler, combine the beeswax, glycerin, almond oil and rose water. Remove from the heat and slowly blend in the soap mixture, stirring continuously until it cools. Stir in the patchouli oil. Store the mixture in a lidded glass jar.

Peppermint Lotion

Invigorate your feet with this minty lotion.

1/2 **cup distilled water**

1 **teaspoon borax powder**

1/3 **cup coconut oil**

1 **tablespoon liquid lanolin**

1 **tablespoon beeswax, grated**

2 **teaspoons sweet almond oil**

25 **drops peppermint oil**

3 **drops red food coloring**

In a pan, boil the water and add the borax, stirring until it is dissolved. In a second pan over low heat, melt the coconut oil, lanolin, beeswax and almond oil until thoroughly blended. Remove from heat. Slowly pour the water and borax mixture into the oils, stirring constantly to avoid lumps. Stir until the mixture thickens and has cooled to the touch. Stir in the peppermint oil and food coloring until thoroughly blended. Store in a lidded bottle or jar.

Bath Oils

There are two kinds of bath oil: Dispersible Bath Oil that mixes with bathwater and Floating Bath Oil that floats on top of the bathwater and coats your skin as you enter and leave the tub.

Dispersible Bath Oil

3 parts Turkey red oil (treated castor oil)

1 part essential oil

Blend the two ingredients, and use 1 teaspoon of the mixture per bath.

Floating Bath Oil

3 parts sweet almond safflower, sunflower or soy oil

1 part essential oil

Blend the ingredients together, and add 2 tablespoons per bath.

Double Citrus Bath Oil

MAKES APPROXIMATELY 1/2 CUP.

6 tablespoons sweet almond oil

10 drops grapefruit oil

10 drops orange oil

Combine all the oils in a bottle with an airtight lid. Shake well.

Use about 1 teaspoon in your bathwater. Because the oil floats on top of the water as you get out of the bath, your skin will be coated with a clean scent of citrus.

Perfume Oils

You can create a signature scent that's all your own, or create one for a friend. You can mix any of the essential oils for a unique combination—the oils are inexpensive enough to experiment.

5 drops essential oil of your choosing

1 tablespoon treated castor oil

In a small bowl, add the drops of essential oil to the castor oil and stir. Store the mixture in a small glass vial or a clean perfume bottle.

Simple Massage Oil

This makes a great oil to pamper yourself or your partner.

2 ounces almond oil

20 to 30 drops essential oil of your choice

4 drops wheat germ oil

Blend all the ingredients, and place in a dark, lidded bottle. (The wheat germ will preserve the freshness.)

Pour a little of the oil into the palms of your hands and rub into the skin. Be sure to keep it away from your eyes.

Herbal Footbath Bags

Are your feet barking at you? Soothe your dogs
with some herbal comfort.

MAKES 2 BAGS.

I tablespoon dried comfrey

I tablespoon lavender

I tablespoon pennyroyal

I tablespoon rosemary

I tablespoon sage

2 (10-inch) muslin squares

2 (12-inch) lengths of cord

In a large plastic bowl, blend all the dried herbs. Let these stand covered for 48 hours. Divide the mixture into two equal portions, and put in the middle of the muslin squares. Draw the edges of the squares together, and tie shut with the cord.

Boil a gallon of water on the stove. Remove from heat and place one of the footbath bags in the water. Let steep until cool enough to handle, about 15 minutes. Pour the mixture in a plastic pan, large enough to soak both feet.

Bath Bag Scrub

This makes a wonderfully invigorating but mild
scrub. The oatmeal softens the skin and the cornmeal cleanses, so you
can chose either or both together.

3 tablespoons oatmeal or cornmeal

3 tablespoons dried herbs

12-inch square of tulle

16 inches pretty ribbon

Combine the meal and herbs in a small bowl. Pour into the middle of the tulle square. Draw the corners together, and tie securely with the ribbon. Use in the bath or shower as an all-over body scrub.

Water for Your
Charley Horse

Muscles need to relax and take comfort. Let them
enjoy this special water.

2 teaspoons grated fresh gingerroot

1 pint mineral water

In a pan, heat the gingerroot and water over medium heat until it boils. Remove from stove, cover and let steep until the water turns deep yellow, or about 5 to 10 minutes.

Draw a hot bath, and pour the mixture in it. Soak your aching muscles.

Quick Footbath Cooler

This is the quickest way to give your feet quick relief.
The cold water combined with the lavender quickly shocks your
feet into a blissful state.

1 gallon cold water

3 drops lavender essential oil

Pour the cold water in a dishpan and add the essential oil. Stir. Place your feet in the water and soak for 10 minutes.

Milk Bath

This bath mixture is a wonderful yet somewhat expensive indulgence for the body. The combination of ingredients will make your skin feel milky soft.

2 cups honey

3 quarts buttermilk

1 cup bicarbonate of soda

1 cup kosher salt

Heat the honey and buttermilk in a large pan over low heat until the honey is dissolved. Fill the tub with water as hot as you can stand and add the soda and salt. Then slowly add the milk and honey mixture. Soak in bath for 10 minutes. Enjoy!

Muscle Spice

This is a simple yet very effective balm for tired, achy muscles.

1 tablespoon ground cayenne pepper

1 pint apple cider vinegar

Mix the pepper and vinegar in a pan on medium heat until slightly boiling. Remove from heat and let cool to room temperature. Bottle the mixture while it is still warm in a glass container.

In a microwave-safe container, warm the mixture in the microwave for 2 minutes on low heat. Soak a towel with the mixture, then heat the towel in the microwave. Apply the towel directly to your tired muscles.

Peel-Away-the-Day Bath Bags

MAKES 6 BATH BAGS.

1 ounce rose petals	2 bay leaves, broken
1 ounce lavender flowers	1 ounce crushed rosemary
2 tablespoons rolled oats	6 (10-inch) muslin squares
1/2 ounce cut orange peel	6 (12-inch) lengths of cord
1/2 ounce cut lemon peel	

In a lidded container, shake all the ingredients together. Place 2 tablespoons of the mixture in the middle of a muslin square. Draw the edges of the square together and tie shut with the cord. Hang the bag on the faucet as the water fills your tub, then throw the bag in the water while you bathe.

Bubble Bags

This bath bag will create a lovely lather as you use it. You and your kids will love it because it is such a pleasure for you and fun for them.

3 tablespoons oatmeal or cornmeal

3 tablespoons dried herbs

3 tablespoons grated Ivory soap

12-inch square of tulle

16 inches satin ribbon

Combine oatmeal or cornmeal, dried herbs and soap in a small bowl. Pour mixture into the middle of the tulle square. Draw the corners together, and knot securely with the satin ribbon. Use this instead of soap and a washcloth.

Breakfast Bran for Bath Bags

Bran is not just for breakfast anymore.

3 (10-inch) diameter muslin circles

9 tablespoons bran

1 tablespoon lavender flowers

1 tablespoon chamomile flowers

1 tablespoon rosemary tips

3 small rubber bands

3 (1-foot) pieces of decorative ribbon

In the center of each circle of muslin, place 3 tablespoons of bran. Add the lavender flowers to one, chamomile flowers to the second and rosemary tips to the third. Gather the outer edge of the material, and close with a rubber band. Tie with the decorative ribbon. Use these bath bags like scrubbies, or hang them under the spout as the water fills your tub.

Bath Beads

These bath beads will release a heavenly aroma of roses
as they moisturize.

¹/₄ **cup powdered milk**

3 tablespoons white flour

3 tablespoons borax powder

¹/₄ **cup rose water**

2 teaspoons mineral oil

15 drops rose fragrance oil

1 drop red food coloring

In a nonreactive bowl, blend the milk, flour and borax. Add the rose water, mineral oil, rose fragrance oil and food coloring. Stir until the consistency is that of cookie dough. By teaspoons, roll the "dough" into balls. Place the balls on a sheet of tinfoil or waxed paper and allow to dry uncovered for 24 hours.

Drop 1 or 2 beads in a warm bath.

Salty Essentials

Bath salts calm and soothe tired, aching muscles. Treat yourself with a peaceful moment in a hot tub.

2 cups Epsom salts

30 drops of your favorite essential oil

5 to 8 drops food coloring

Pour the Epsom salt into a wide-mouth jar and add the essential oil. Stir vigorously. Stir in the food coloring, mixing thoroughly until the color is evenly distributed. Cover tightly and let stand for three weeks, stirring every 2 to 3 days.

Sprinkle 1 teaspoon in a hot bath.

Peppermint Bath Salts

1 cup Epsom salts

1 teaspoon peppermint oil

2 drops red food coloring

Grind up the Epsom salt to a fine powder in a food processor. In a bowl, mix the salts, peppermint oil and food coloring until thoroughly blended. Spread the mixture evenly on a baking sheet and let dry overnight. Store in a lidded jar.

Pour 2 tablespoons in your bathwater and relax.

Fizzing Bath Salts

*The kitchen can be a source of many things. If you are out
of food coloring, add some unsweetened powdered drink mix to
colorize the bath salts.*

MAKES 8 TREATMENTS.

1 cup baking soda

1 cup cornstarch

2 tablespoons citric acid

2 (1-ounce) packages of your favorite color of unsweetened concentrated powdered

drink mix

In a bowl, mix all ingredients together. Fill small plastic resealable bags
with 1/4 cup of the salts for individual treatments.

Bath Crystals

This recipe makes 1 cup of crystals, but simply multiply the ingredients proportionately to make as much as you want. And you'll want to make lots for yourself and for gifts. You start this sophisticated concoction with the most humble of ingredients, rock salt, like the kind used in an ice-cream maker.

1 cup coarse rock salt

2 to 3 drops food coloring of your choice

20 to 25 drops essential oil of your choice

Place rock salt in a wide-mouth container with a lid. For each cup of salt, add 2 or 3 drops of food coloring. Mix with a spoon or shake well. Add 2 or 3 more drops of food coloring at a time, and continue mixing until desired color is reached. To the colored crystals, add 20 to 25 drops of essential oils, mixing or shaking well. Keep in a tightly closed jar or the oil will quickly evaporate. Use 1 or 2 heaping tablespoons in a hot tub.

Bath Salts Sundae

This is the ultimate gift for a friend on a diet.
This has the look of great food for inside the tummy but is great
enjoyment for outside the tummy. You'll need a tall, clear,
ice-cream sundae glass to achieve the full effect, but
any tall glass will work.

8 ounces cornstarch

8 ounces citric acid

16 ounces baking soda

8 to 10 drops essential oil of your choice

Food coloring of your choice

White net scrubby

One large red bead

Double-sided tape

Preheat oven to 200 degrees F. Blend the first five ingredients thoroughly and pour onto a cookie sheet. Put the cookie sheet in the oven for 15 minutes, stirring occasionally, until the mixture is completely dry. Spoon the mixture into the ice-cream sundae dish and fill to the top.

Lay the white scrubby on top of the salt-filled sundae dish, attach the red bead to the top of the scrubby with a small piece of double-sided tape (this simulates a cherry on top of whipped cream). The remaining mixture can be stored in an airtight container.

Bath Vinegar

This vinegar mixture makes for a wonderfully fragrant
and refreshing bath.

2 cups rose petals

4 cups apple cider vinegar

1 cup bottled springwater

In a lidded jar, steep the petals and vinegar for about 8 weeks. Strain and rebottle, adding the water. Allow the mixture to blend for a few days.

Use 1 cup in bathwater, pouring it under the tap as you fill the tub.

Lavender Bubbly

Lavender is known for its cooling and relaxing qualities.
This bubble bath makes a thoughtful yet inexpensive gift to give
a friend who's overstressed!

I large bundle lavender

I large bottle clear organic, unscented shampoo

10 drops lavender oil

Put the bundle of lavender head down in a clean, screw-top jar. All you really need are the flower blossoms, so cut off any long stalks. Add the shampoo and the lavender oil. Close the jar and place it in a sunny windowsill for 3 to 4 weeks, shaking daily. Strain the blossoms and rebottle the liquid.

Hobo Bubble Bath

*Use this inexpensive mixture to create a luxurious, soothing bubble
bath. The almond oil will moisten your skin, and the dishwashing soap
creates glorious bubbles.*

2 tablespoons almond oil

8 ounces mild, unscented dishwashing soap

Blend the oil with the dishwashing soap and pour
into a lidded bottle. Use about 1 ounce for each bath.

Sweet Bubble Bath

A bubbly bath can be so sweet. All you have to do is add a little
sugar to extend the life of your bubbles.

¼ cup glycerin

I cup mild dishwashing liquid, such as Ivory

I teaspoon sugar

50 drops of your favorite fragrance oil

Combine all the ingredients and put into a squeeze or pump bottle. Use 2 to 3 tablespoons per bath.

Floral Water

This is a refreshing face splash.

12 tablespoons rose water

2 tablespoons witch hazel

5 drops rose essential oil

Mix all the ingredients together and store in a lidded glass bottle. It will last several months.

Splash on your face after cleansing.

Meal-Milk Sachet

MAKES APPROXIMATELY 8 SACHETS.

I cup dry oatmeal

3/4 cup powdered milk

1/2 cup dried lavender buds

1/2 cup dried, crumbled peppermint leaves

8 (5-inch) squares of gauze

8 (12-inch) pieces of ribbon

Blend all the ingredients in a plastic bowl. Pour 2 tablespoons of the mixture in the middle of the gauze square, and tie up the corners with the ribbon.

Hang the sachet under the faucet while you fill the tub, then toss it into the water for a luxurious bath.

Linen Refresher

*This aromatic mixture lends a refreshing scent
to your linens and clothes.*

$^1/_2$ cup anise

I cup crushed bay leaves

I cup crushed eucalyptus leaves

$^1/_2$ cup dried lemon verbena

$^1/_2$ cup crushed lavender

Combine all the ingredients and place the mixture in a box with small perforations in the sides. Place the container between the linens or on the shelf beside them. You can also use some of this mixture in a perforated envelope and tuck it in the sides of your suitcase or in your clothing drawers.

Scrubby Sponge

1 yard 8-inch wide bridal tulle

1 yard thin satin ribbon

Lay the tulle on a flat surface. Fan fold it in layers that are 3 inches wide. Tie the middle of the folded material with the ribbon. Secure the tied ribbon by tacking the folds together with a needle and thread. Fluff the folded tulle into a nice round ball.

CHAPTER FOUR

Perfect Potpourri Potions

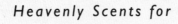

Heavenly Scents for

Your Home

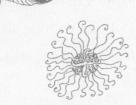

Canning Jar Potpourri

This mixture will provide a wonderful air freshener. A scrap of netting or fabric over the opening of the container, secured with the outside ring of a canning jar lid is an ideal way to use this. Simply remove the inner circle of the lid whenever you want to release the aroma.

2 tablespoons ground cinnamon

1 tablespoon ground cloves

24 drops essential oil of your choice

1 cup cedar chips or shavings

1 cup sandalwood chips

1 cup dried mint leaves

1 cup lavender

1 cup dried marigold petals

1 cup dried tea roses or petals

Mix the cinnamon and cloves and place on the bottom of a 16-ounce canning jar. Add 12 drops of essential oil to this mixture. Layer the next six ingredients one at a time in the jar. Complete the jar by adding the remaining drops of essential oil. Place a lid on the jar and let it sit for about 2 weeks.

Christmas Potpourri

This seasonal potpourri will add a wonderful scent to your home when placed in any room in a decorative bowl or simmered in a pot of water on the stove. Be sure to turn the stove off before you go out caroling!

6 oranges

Handful of cloves

2 ounces orange oil

10 drops cinnamon essential oil

12 cinnamon sticks

With a vegetable peeler, peel long strips of skin from the oranges. Stud the peels with the cloves. Place in a wide-mouth lidded jar. Add orange oil, cinnamon oil and cinnamon sticks into the jar and let sit for 2 weeks, shaking every few days.

Floral Bouquet Potpourri

This mixture looks and smells as sweet and fresh as a spring bouquet. It uses no dried ground spice because they would discolor the delicate blossoms.

I cup dried lily of the valley flowers

I cup dried white fuchsia flowers

I cup dried lavender leaves, crumbled

I cup dried white miniature roses

4 tablespoons dried orrisroot powder

6 drops orange blossom oil

6 drops lily of the valley oil

Mix all the ingredients together in a large lidded container and set aside for 6 weeks. Gently stir the contents daily to distribute evenly.

TIP: To dry flowers, simply cut the stems just above the ground. Bundle 10 to 12 flowers together with a piece of twine. Hang upside down in a dark, dry place for about 3 months. Gently snip the flower heads from the stems to be used for potpourri.

French Garden Potpourri

You don't have to get on an airplane to enjoy a year in Provence.

1 cup dried lavender flowers

1 cup dried dianthus

1 cup dried rose petals

1 cup dried scented geranium leaves

1 tablespoon ground cinnamon

2 teaspoons ground allspice

1 teaspoon dried grated lemon peel

2 tablespoons dried orrisroot powder

5 drops rose oil

Mix all the ingredients together in a lidded container and set aside for 6 weeks. Gently stir daily to distribute the fragrances.

Fruity Potpourri

You can use this heady potpourri all year 'round, but place a handful into a muslin bag or sachet and it makes a perfect decoration for your Christmas gifts.

I cup dried apples, cubed

4 cinnamon sticks, broken

I whole nutmeg, broken

2 tablespoons whole allspice

I cup whole dried cranberries

2 tablespoons whole cloves

In a plastic lidded container, blend all the ingredients. Cover and store. When ready to use, place in a decorative bowl or muslin bag for use.

Jelly-Jar Potpourri

This easy-to-make potpourri is subtle but lasts a very long time. Simply take off the lid whenever you want to release the scent. Liquid potpourri is available at craft stores in a variety of scents.

1 cup liquid potpourri

2 packages Knox gelatin

Heat 1/2 cup liquid potpourri in medium saucepan, then stir in the gelatin until dissolved. Remove from heat and stir in the remaining liquid potpourri. Fill a decorative 5-ounce lidded jar with the mixture. To speed up the gelling process, cover and refrigerate for about 2 hours.

Just-Beyond-the-Trees Potpourri

This mixture makes a beautiful display for both sight and smell, and a wonderful hostess gift.

1 cup whole nutmegs, cracked

1 cup mini Indian corn*

2 cups maple, oak and elm leaves

1 cup poppy seed heads*

1/2 cup cloves

1/2 cup coriander seeds

1 teaspoon patchouli essential oil

1 teaspoon nutmeg oil

*The Indian corn and poppy seed heads are generally available in the fall in craft and grocery stores.

Blend all the ingredients in a large lidded container. Let the mixture set for 2 to 3 weeks. Gently shake to help blend the fragrances daily. When ready to use, display in a decorative bowl anywhere in the house.

Mint Scents Potpourri

The colonists claimed that mint potpourri "cleared the head," so they placed it in dishes or jars by their desks.

2 cups dried peppermint

2 cups dried orange mint

2 cups dried spearmint leaves

2 cups dried lavender blossoms

I cup dried thyme

I cup dried rosemary leaves

$1/2$ cup orrisroot

I tablespoon oil of lavender

Combine all the ingredients in a large lidded container. Set aside for 5 to 6 weeks, gently stirring every few days.

Pine Potpourri

You don't have to save this pine-fresh scent for Christmastime.
It'll bring the great outdoors into your home year 'round.

2 quarts ground pine needles

I cup orrisroot

I tablespoon pine oil

Blend the pine needles in the food processor and pour into a lidded plastic container. Add the orrisroot and pine oil and mix thoroughly. Let sit for 5 to 6 weeks. Every 2 or 3 days, shake the container to mix.

Pomander

*Pomanders have long been used as a means to bring fragrance
in the home as they tend to have a lasting scent. You can string
a cord or ribbon through the ball and hang it in a closet or cabinet.*

3 ounces ground cinnamon

3 ounces ground cloves

1/2 ounce ground allspice

1/2 ounce grated nutmeg

1/2 ounce ground coriander

1 ounce orrisroot

6 Seville oranges

4 ounces whole cloves

Blend the cinnamon, cloves, allspice, nutmeg, coriander and orrisroot thoroughly in a lidded earthenware dish large enough to hold all the oranges. Using a toothpick to make a hole, stud the oranges with the cloves. Roll the oranges in the powdered mixture and leave them in the spices. Cover the dish and let stand in a warm place. You should roll the pomanders in the spice mixture daily. Should the spice mixture begin to feel damp, leave the lid partially off so the moisture can evaporate. After about 4 to 5 weeks, the oranges will have shrunk and hardened and the pomanders will be ready to package or use.

Potpourri's Ugly Stepsister

This is an inexpensive potpourri. The absorbent kitty litter holds the scent fabulously. But kitty litter isn't very attractive, so you might want to put the scented kitty litter in a bowl and cover with flowers or pour it into a colored vase. You can also make cloth bags and fill them to use as sachets or scented pillows.

Kitty litter (the cheaper the better)
Essential oil of your choice

Pour the kitty litter into a large plastic lidded container. For every cup of kitty litter, add 15 drops of essential oil. Let stand for 4 to 6 weeks, stirring every other day.

Rose Jar Potpourri

Create a rose potpourri that makes a beautiful gift for a friend.

2 cups dried rose petals

1/4 cup kosher salt

1/4 ounce each ground cloves, mace and allspice

1/2 ounce ground cinnamon

1/4 pound lavender flowers

1/4 cup toilet water

10 drops rose essential oil

2 ounces ground orrisroot

Mix rose petals and the salt, then stir in the spices, lavender flowers, toilet water, oil and orrisroot. Pour the mixture into a lidded plastic container and let sit for 4 to 5 weeks, stirring occasionally. Display in a decorative bowl.

Scents of Autumn Potpourri

This special seasonal potpourri looks and smells wonderful
when displayed in a dried gourd.

I tablespoon freshly ground pepper

I tablespoon freshly ground
    coriander

I teaspoon ground ginger

I teaspoon ground nutmeg

20 drops ginger oil

20 drops lime oil

6 drops basil oil

6 drops juniper oil

8 cups dried filler ingredients (rose
    petals, rosebuds, oak leaves,
    acorns, seed heads, small
    pinecones, dried tree bark,
    small corncobs)

In a small bowl, mix the pepper, coriander, ginger and nutmeg together. Add the ginger, lime, basil and juniper oils to create a moist powder. Place the mixture in a large bowl with the filler ingredients and toss to blend thoroughly. Store in an airtight container for 5 to 6 weeks, stirring every 2 to 3 days.

Specialize to Vaporize

You can create seasonal vapor flavors: summer citrus, autumn ginger, winter cinnamon or spring rose! The possibilities are limited only by your imagination and the essential oils you can find.

Essential oil of your choosing

Water

Blend 25 drops of oil with 3 cups water. Simmer in a pot on the stove at the lowest heat or place in an electric warmer. Don't forget to check the water level every 15 minutes. (It's always good to set the stove timer to remind you.)

Stove-Top Potpourri

Not only will this fill your house with the most aromatic aroma,
it will help open up a stuffy head!

1 cup dried peppermint leaves

1 cup cinnamon stick pieces

Mix the ingredients together and store in a lidded container.

Use 3 tablespoons of the spice mixture for 4 cups of water. Simmer on the stove over low heat. Check the water level every 15 minutes or so. (Set your stove timer as a reminder.)

Sunshine Potpourri

This sparkling mixture can be refreshed easily by periodically adding additional essential oils. It is also a perfect gift when packaged in a corsage bag, available from florists, and tied with a pretty bow.

4 teaspoons ground cinnamon

1 tablespoon ground orrisroot

1 whole nutmeg, grated

45 drops lavender oil

45 drops rose geranium oil

15 drops citrus oil

8 cups dried flower petals and heads (rose petals, rosebuds, peonies, lavender)

In a small bowl, mix the cinnamon, orrisroot and nutmeg. Add the lavender, rose geranium and citrus oils to create a moist powder. In a large mixing bowl, pour the powder mixture onto the flower parts and petals. Toss to blend thoroughly. Place the potpourri mixture in a lidded container for 5 to 6 weeks. Every 2 to 3 days, stir the potpourri.

Woodstove Potpourri

*This is a wonderful potpourri to package in a corsage bag,
tie on a decorative scoop and give to a friend.*

1/2 cup whole cloves

1/2 cup whole allspice

1/2 cup whole coriander

1/2 cup broken cinnamon sticks

1/2 cup dried orange peel pieces

1/2 cup dried lemon peel

Mix all the ingredients and store in a lidded container.

To use: Place a small pan of water on the stove to simmer. Pour 5 tablespoons of the mixture in the water. Let it simmer.

Caution: Don't forget to check the pan regularly. The water may evaporate and scorch the pan. A stove timer set for 15 minutes is a good reminder.

Woodsy Earth Potpourri

Bring the great outdoors indoors with this forest mix.

I cup dried lime seedpods

I cup cedar bark shavings

I cup sandalwood shavings

I cup small pinecones

I tablespoon whole cloves

I tablespoon star anise

I stick cinnamon, crushed

2 tablespoons dried orrisroot powder

5 drops sandalwood oil

Mix all the ingredients together in a large lidded container and set aside for 6 weeks. Stir the contents daily to distribute the spices evenly.

CHAPTER FIVE

Mixtures to Minimize Maintenance

Cleaners, Fresheners,

Polishes and Repellents

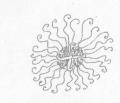

All-Purpose Household Cleanser

This gentle cleanser provides grease-cutting power and a pleasant fragrance, too. It is to only be used on kitchen and bathroom surfaces—no wood.

MAKES APPROXIMATELY 1 QUART.

I quart warm water

I teaspoon biodegradable liquid soap

I teaspoon borax

Juice of I lemon

Combine all ingredients in a large clean spray or squeeze bottle. Shake well before each use.

Copper Cleaner

If you have an herb garden, this is an inexpensive way to clean copper.

Fresh sorrel leaves

To bring the shine back to a copper pot or container, scrub the wet pot with a handful of fresh leaves.

Gritty Scrub Hand Cleanser

*This hand cleanser is great to keep at your kitchen sink
or in your washroom.*

1 cup grated all-natural soap

1 cup cornmeal

¼ cup chopped almonds

4 tablespoons corn oil

Pour the soap, cornmeal and almonds into a food processor and pulse to create a fine meal. In a microwave-proof container, combine the meal with the corn oil, mix, cover loosely with waxed paper and microwave on low power for 90 seconds. Repeat this process until you have a paste smooth enough for the container of your choice. (If you want to pour the hand cleaner into a pump dispenser, add more oil until the right consistency is reached.) This cleanser will last 3 to 4 weeks.

Herbal Tea Spray Cleaner

*This is a terrific and nose-friendly cleaner for most surfaces,
except glass (the oils will leave a residue). It is always best to test
any cleanser in hidden areas before completely washing the
whole surface, including wood.*

1 teaspoon borax

2 tablespoons white vinegar

2 cups hot water

1/4 teaspoon eucalyptus essential oil

1/4 teaspoon lavender essential oil

3 drops tea tree essential oil

Mix all the ingredients together and stir until the dry ingredients dissolve.
Pour the mixture into a spray bottle. Scrub and rinse with a clean, damp cloth.

Hoo Doo Mildew

A wash that is most useful for a lot of household surfaces.

2 gallons water

2 cups chlorine bleach

I cup powdered laundry detergent

I cup powdered dishwashing detergent

Mix all the ingredients in a large tub or bucket.

Using a stiff brush, scrub wooden decks, wood siding or patio furniture with liberal amounts of Hoo Doo. Rinse well with clean water. Don't forget to wear rubber gloves, as the bleach can be hard on your hands.

Lemo-Mint Window Wash

This is not only a fresh-smelling and effective window cleaner, it also fends off flies from perching on your window and leaving those nasty little spots.

Juice of 1 lemon

2 cups club soda

1/2 teaspoon peppermint essential oil

1 teaspoon cornstarch

Mix all the ingredients thoroughly and pour into a plastic spray bottle. Shake well before each use.

No-Pain Drain Cleaner

*This is an efficient method for cleaning drains and
is even safe for septic systems.*

¹/₂ cup baking soda

¹/₂ cup white vinegar or lemon juice

1 quart boiling water

Pour the baking soda down a sluggish drain, followed by the lemon juice
or vinegar. This will create a volcano-like reaction. Don't panic, this is normal.
Let stand in the sink and pipes for 15 minutes, then flush 1 quart of boiling
water down the drain. Repeat if necessary.

Dryer Bags

Have you ever washed a load of clothes, and two days later remembered you forgot to put them in the dryer? Remember the odor that blows you away as you lift the washer lid? Well, this little concoction will keep you from having to rewash the laundry. Simply put the clothes in the dryer with one of the muslin bags and the odor should be gone.

MAKES 6 TO 8 BAGS.

1 cup dry lemon verbena

1 cup dry mint

2 cups cedar shavings

Mix all the ingredients in a lidded container. Let set for about a week. Place handfuls of the mixture in small muslin bags.

Versatile Herb Vinegar

I have discovered five great uses for this herb vinegar.
You will probably find even more.

1. Clean all kinds of glass (The smell is so much more pleasant than straight vinegar you'll be saying "Yes, I do windows, with pleasure.")

2. Spray on your dog to combat odor (Be sure to avoid the face.)

3. Spritz on a salad

4. Spritz on your body if you get a little sunburned

5. Dip a piece of cheesecloth in the mixture, wring it out and wrap it around cheese to prevent molding

1 cup mixed fresh herbs (mint, chives, basil, parsley), finely chopped

2 cups white wine vinegar

Place the herbs in a heat-resistant lidded jar. Warm the vinegar and pour it over the herbs. Steep for 3 weeks, shaking the jar every other day. Strain and pour into a spray bottle.

Ashtrays That Smell Good

*A perfect alternative to regular ashtrays, this recipe helps
to diffuse the odor of old cigar butts as well as helping to
mask the smoke in the air.*

White sand

Baking soda

Essential oils

Pour equal parts white sand and baking soda into decorative bowls or deep-dish ashtrays. Pour a few drops of your favorite essential oil and blend.

Carpet Sprinkle

A sprinkle a day keeps the stinky away.

1 cup baking soda

1 cup cornstarch

20 drops lavender oil

20 drops rose oil

In a bowl, mix all the ingredients. Place in an old talc container or any can or jar with a pierced lid so you can sprinkle the mixture.

About once a week, especially if you have pets, sprinkle this mixture on your carpet and let sit for about 10 minutes. Then vacuum it up. This not only replaces the "just-been-vacuumed" smell and masks unpleasant pet smells, the warmth of the vacuum increases the scent and carries it into the air.

Customized Air Freshener

This is a distinctive air freshener that you can create to your own liking. Experiment and create different scents. Gently spray a few squirts into the air and enjoy.

Essential oil of your choosing

Water

Using a ratio of 12 drops oil to 8 tablespoons water, pour ingredients into a spray bottle. Shake before each use.

Decorative Doggy Deodorizer

Accessorize your pooch with a beneficial bandanna.

$^1/_2$ **cup baking soda**

2 cups water

Large bandanna (depending on the size of your pooch)

Stir the baking soda into the water until dissolved. Thoroughly soak the bandanna in the water mixture. Let dry in the sunshine. It is always easier if you do 2 or 3 at a time.

Tie the bandanna around your dog's neck. The baking soda will help absorb most doggy odor.

Recycled Dryer Sheets

Even clean clothing or blankets that have been in the drawer or closet too long need to be refreshed. Recycled dryer sheets are an excellent way to do just that. After the initial use of the dryer sheet, the properties of reducing static cling are essentially gone, so their only value now is to provide fresh scent.

Used dryer sheets

Essential oil of your choice

10 cotton balls

Save used dryer sheets in a lidded plastic container. After you have 5 or 6, place a couple drops of essential oil on each of the cotton balls, and place them in the container with the dryer sheets. After about 2 weeks the sheets should be scented enough to use.

Throw a scented sheet into your dryer to give your clothes and linens a nice pleasant smell. The sheets can generally be recycled about 3 times before they become too thin to hold together.

No-Buff Furniture Polish

¹/₂ cup linseed oil

¹/₂ cup malt vinegar

I teaspoon lemon oil

I teaspoon lime oil

Pour the linseed oil and vinegar into a lidded jar and close tightly. Shake well to mix. Add the lemon and lime oils and shake again. Pour into a spray bottle.

Spray a fine mist of the polish on a soft dusting cloth (cloth diapers are great). Lightly dust or polish your furniture.

Old-Time Furniture Polish

This polish will clean wood surfaces and provide a beautiful shine. The turpentine cuts through dirt and grime. Always test the wood surface in a hidden area first to ensure the wood will not be stained or damaged.

1/2 cup natural beeswax

3/4 cup pure turpentine

25 drops cedarwood oil

12 drops sandalwood oil

Grate the beeswax and place it in an 8-ounce screw-top jar. Pour the turpentine over the beeswax and screw on the lid. Let this sit for about a week or until the two ingredients become a creamy consistency. Add the essential oils and blend thoroughly.

Apply a thin coating of the polish with a clean, soft cloth, rub into the furniture and let dry for a few minutes. Buff vigorously with a clean cloth to a deep, lustrous shine.

Furniture Wax

This paste wax cleans and polishes wood surfaces while instilling a protective coating. Always test the wood surface in a hidden area before completely polishing. With a clean cotton cloth, use a circular motion to rub the wax onto the wooden surfaces. Then buff with sheep's wool or a soft cotton cloth.

1/4 cup carnauba wax

2 tablespoons beeswax

1 1/4 cups olive oil

1 teaspoon lavender essential oil

Melt the carnauba wax and the beeswax in a double boiler over low heat. Remove from heat and stir in the olive oil and lavender oil. Pour mixture into a wide-mouth lidded tin or glass container. The wax will harden as it cools.

Wood Furniture Scratch Removal

Sometimes there are easy ways to diminish flaws
we create in our furniture.

Camphor oil

Scratches can be filled on light or dark wood by rubbing them with camphor oil. Apply with a soft cloth, and rub in the direction of the grain of the wood. The darker the wood, the more oil you need to apply.

Scratch Ointment

You know all those little cuts and scrapes you always get while working in the yard, flower bed or vegetable garden? This is a great ointment to use to soothe your skin.

6 tablespoons white petroleum jelly

1/2 teaspoon paraffin wax

1/4 teaspoon anhydrous lanolin

12 drops lavender essential oil

Place the petroleum jelly, paraffin wax and anhydrous lanolin in a double boiler and melt slowly over low heat. Once it has all dissolved, remove from the heat and continue blending the mixture as it cools and thickens. Slowly stir in the essential oil and store in a lidded glass container.

Rub a small amount of the ointment on minor cuts or abrasions.

Bug-Off Spray

Unlike most commercial bug repellents, this one has a very pleasant odor. (This spray can also be used sparingly on carpets to repel fleas. Yeah!)

10 drops pennyroyal

10 drops eucalyptus

20 drops citronella oil

15 drops cedarwood oil

1 teaspoon jojoba oil

Combine all the ingredients in a spray bottle. Shake well before each use.

Spray a thin layer on the skin that is exposed to bugs.

Note: Test spray on a small hidden area of carpet or clothing to ensure no reaction to color dyes. Never saturate carpet, only spray lightly.

Furry Friend Flea Dip

6 tablespoons Joy or Dawn dishwashing soap

(stick to these brands)

6 tablespoons glycerin

2¹/₂ tablespoons white vinegar

I quart water

Mix all ingredients in a clean plastic bottle or milk jug. This mixture will keep for several months.

Get the pooch nice and wet. Pour on a generous amount of the shampoo and lather well. Scrub his coat and skin. For best results, leave the shampoo on the dog for 15 minutes. Rinse and repeat if you desire. This should smother the fleas and give some needed relief to your four-legged friend.

Herb Bug Repellents

Pennyroyal

To repel fleas, mosquitoes and moths, rub some leaves on your skin (not your face) or put some dried leaves in a cloth bag and put it in your pet's bed.

Tansy and Catnip

To repel ants, plant tansy or catnip around the foundation of your home. Ants do not like to pass through it.

Clover Flowers and Basil

To repel houseflies, place a sprig or bouquet of clover flowers or basil in your kitchen, and the flies will stay away.

Bay Leaves

To repel weevils, place a whole bay leaf in the top of your containers of flour, cornmeal and other grains. It will not flavor the food but will keep the weevils out.

Recipes for Your Mice

To repel mice, place long stems of mint leaves along the eaves in your attic or grow mint plants along the base of your home. The mice will frown on the scent and seek a home elsewhere.

To attract the little rodent to your trap, you would think cheese would be the best bait... but a few anise seeds mixed with peanut butter is far more effective.

CHAPTER SIX

Recipes to Spice Up Your Toiletries

Personal Products

Including Cleansers, Shower Gel,

Facials and Shampoos

Cocoa Cleanser

*The scent of chocolate is always welcome. So why not
make a hand cleanser that smells like fudge?*

1 cup distilled water

¼ cup unscented shampoo concentrate

½ teaspoon table salt

1½ teaspoons powdered cocoa

15 drops vanilla essential oil

In a small nonreactive saucepan, heat the water and shampoo concentrate
over medium heat until it is dissolved. Add the salt, cocoa and vanilla essential
oil. Stir until thick and thoroughly blended. Store in a squeeze or lidded bottle.

Glycerin Hand Wash

Create your own unique hand wash. This is also
a thoughtful gift for a friend.

1 cup distilled water

1 tablespoon unscented glycerin soap

20 drops of your favorite essential oil fragrance

In a small pan, boil the water and the glycerin soap until it is liquefied. Remove the pan from heat and stir in the essential oil. Let the mixture cool and store in a pump or squeeze bottle.

Shower Gel

3/4 cup distilled water

1/4 cup unscented shampoo

1 teaspoon table salt

20 drops of your favorite essential oil scent

In a small pan, heat the water and the shampoo until completely liquefied over medium heat. Add the salt and stir until the mixture is well-blended and thickened. Stir in the essential oil. Let cool, then pour into a squeeze or pump bottle.

Slime-Me-Clean Shower Gel

*Children will enjoy bathing with a gel that looks like
it might make you dirty.*

I cup distilled water

2 tablespoons unscented shampoo concentrate

I teaspoon table salt

20 drops citrus essential oil

2 drops green food coloring

In a small nonreactive saucepan, heat the water and shampoo over medium heat until it is dissolved. Add the salt, citrus oil and food coloring. Stir until thick and thoroughly blended. Store in a squeeze bottle.

Soft Soap

1 cup hot water

1 cup grated pure soap (takes about 1 bar) or 1 cup soap flakes

Heat the water in a medium microwave-proof dish. Remove from microwave oven. Stir in the soap and return to the oven on high power for 90 seconds to bring to a boil. Remove and stir again until the soap is completely dissolved. Store in a pump or squeeze bottle.

VARIATIONS: Add several drops of your favorite essential oil or perfume to the basic recipe, or to make a creamier version, add 2 tablespoons olive or almond oil to the basic recipe.

The Bee's Knees Cold Cream

This is similar to the traditional commercial cold cream, used to cleanse and smooth the skin.

Fifty-five ounces white beeswax

1/2 cup almond oil

1/2 teaspoon borax

1/3 cup rose water

Place the beeswax in a double boiler and add the almond oil. Over low heat, melt the wax, stirring constantly to mix the ingredients. Remove from heat. In a small bowl, dissolve the borax in the rose water and slowly pour it into the melted wax and oil, stirring constantly. It will quickly turn milky and thicken. Continue mixing while it cools. Once it has thickened, pour into a glass jar or lidded container.

Facial Scrub

This gentle facial scrub is mild and aromatic but really refreshing.

MAKES 7 TREATMENTS.

3 bars of Ivory soap, grated

1 cup dried chamomile

3/4 cup dried sage leaves

1 cup oatmeal flakes

Blend all the ingredients together thoroughly. Place 2 tablespoons of the mixture in the center of the double layer of a 4-inch square of cheesecloth. Bring the corners up and tie off with a ribbon. Moisten both the cheesecloth bag and your face. Then with a gentle circular motion, scrub your face with the bag. Rinse with warm water.

Store the remaining mixture in a plastic lidded container. You can reuse the cheesecloth by rinsing and letting it dry after each use.

Lemon-Mint Face Wash

1 cup mineral water

$1/2$ tablespoon unscented glycerin soap

5 drops lemon oil

5 drops peppermint oil

In a pan, boil the water and the glycerin soap until completely liquefied. Remove the pan from heat and add the lemon and peppermint oils and stir. Let cool and bottle.

Aftershave

This is an invigorating aftershave treat.

1 pint cider vinegar

2 cups chopped leaves of fresh thyme, sage, rosemary, basil, dill or lavender

In a medium saucepan, bring the vinegar to a boil and add the chopped leaves. Remove from heat, pour into a lidded jar and let steep for 2 weeks. Strain through a coffee filter. Discard leaves. Store liquid in a lidded jar.

Aftershave Splash with a Punch

This will be a real wake-up for any man.

2 cups witch hazel

3 tablespoons apple cider

1 ounce dried lavender flowers

1 ounce dried peppermint leaves

Blend all the ingredients in a large lidded jar. Close the jar and let the mixture steep for 1 week. Shake daily. Strain, discard the herbs and bottle the liquid.

911 Shampoo

*Somebody just used the last bit of shampoo. You are not
in the mood to run to the market, so why not go in the kitchen
and make your own?*

I cup water

4 tablespoons dishwashing liquid

I teaspoon table salt

I teaspoon mineral oil

15 drops of your favorite essential oil

In a small nonreactive saucepan, heat the water and the dishwashing liquid
over medium heat. Gradually add the salt and mineral oil until the mixture
begins to thicken, stirring constantly. Add the essential oil and bottle.

All-Natural Hair Spray

¹/₂ cup distilled water

2 tablespoons light corn syrup

15 drops fragrance oil (optional)

In a small nonreactive saucepan, bring the water to a boil, then stir in the corn syrup until dissolved. Remove from heat and stir in the fragrance oil. Let cool and store in a spray bottle.

Lemon Hair Spray

*This is an all-natural hair-setting spray for all
types of hair. Apply to dry or wet hair.*

2 lemons, sliced

2 cups water

Place the lemon slices and water in a pan and heat on high until the mixture reaches a rolling boil. Reduce to medium heat until the water is reduced to 1 cup. (About 10 minutes.) Remove from the heat and let cool. Line a strainer with cheesecloth and strain the mixture. Squeeze the cloth thoroughly to get all the juice out. Pour the strained mixture into a pump or spray bottle. The mixture will keep for 1 to 2 months in the refrigerator.

Chamomile Hair Rinse

*This concoction can be used by people with fair hair as a
hair rinse after shampooing. If left in the hair, it may slightly lighten
the color as it dries in the sun. This rinse will leave your hair
shiny and clean.*

4 cups boiling water

3 ounces chamomile flowers

2/3 cup cider vinegar

6 drops chamomile oil

In a large heat-proof container, pour the boiling water over the chamomile flowers, cover and let stand overnight. Strain the liquid. Blend the vinegar and chamomile oil into the chamomile flower liquid and pour into a bottle that has a lid, cork or stopper. After shampooing, massage 4 to 5 tablespoons of rinse into your hair. Rinse with clean water.

Rose Hair Rinse

A pleasant fragrance for your hair.

¼ cup vinegar

1 quart warm water

5 drops rose essential oil

Blend the ingredients, and place in a lidded jar.

Wash your hair with shampoo as usual, and rinse with warm water. Generously saturate hair with Rose Hair Rinse, then rinse again with clean, warm water.

Melted Snow on the Mountain

This mixture should help with an occasional bout of dandruff.
The aspirin cleanses the scalp and hair of dead skin.

1 cup apple cider vinegar

6 aspirins, crushed

$1/4$ cup witch hazel

In a small saucepan, blend all ingredients over medium heat until the aspirin is dissolved. Remove to cool, and store in a lidded jar or bottle.

After shampooing, gently massage rinse into your hair, leave it on for 10 minutes and then rinse again with warm water.

Coco Hair Oil

Sometimes hair that is exposed to the sun consistently can become dry and unruly. A monthly oil treatment will do great things for your hair and scalp.

6 tablespoons coconut oil

4 drops lavender oil

2 drops tea tree oil

2 drops rosemary oil

Mix all the ingredients, and store in a dark glass lidded bottle.

Experiment with the amount of oil that works for your hair. Start with a small dab in the palm of your hands, rub together, and lightly coat your hair with the oil. Gently massage it in. Cover your hair with a moistened, hot towel for 15 minutes, then shampoo.

Hair Hops

Beer always adds a little shine to the hair.

I cup beer

I cup unscented shampoo

In a medium microwave-safe container, heat the beer in the microwave on high for 4 minutes until it reaches a rolling boil. Remove from oven and stir in shampoo. Return to microwave and warm at medium power for 5 minutes until the liquid has been reduced by about a third. Remove from oven and let the mixture cool. This shampoo will last 3 to 4 months.

Use as you would any type of shampoo: Lather, rinse and repeat!

Body Oil

Moisturize your skin with a wonderful body oil.

1 ounce corn oil

1 ounce peanut oil

1 ounce safflower oil

1 ounce wheat germ oil

1 ounce vitamin E (liquid)

4 drops orange oil

3 drops lemon oil

Place all ingredients in a lidded bottle, and shake vigorously to blend. This should last about 4 to 5 months.

Use this concoction just like you would any commercial body oil.

Spray-on Body Oil

This body oil is luxurious and easy to use. The alcohol in the vodka thins the two oils so a fine spray can be achieved.

1 cup vodka

1 cup rose water

6 tablespoons sweet almond oil

2 teaspoons jojoba oil

Mix all ingredients in a small bowl. Store the mixture in a spray bottle. Shake before each use.

Rose Water

Rose water may be used in the bath (about 1 cup), in the hot tub or as a splash after bathing or showering.

2 cups distilled water

1/4 cup vodka

1/2 cup chemical-free rose petals

20 drops rose oil

Combine water, vodka and petals in a clear glass covered jar and place it in the sun. In less than a day, the sun will pull the color and the oils from the petals. Strain through a coffee filter and add the rose oil to the beautiful and fragrant water. Refrigerate in a covered bottle and use within 2 weeks.

Lavender Deodorant Spray

This is a fragrant deodorant spray that won't
irritate the mildest skin.

¹/₄ cup vodka

2 tablespoons witch hazel

15 drops lavender oil

5 drops lemon oil

Combine all ingredients in a spray bottle and shake until well blended.
Always shake before using.

Underarm Deodorant Powder

A powder puff combined with this recipe will make

you feel quite refreshed.

8 tablespoons talcum powder

4 tablespoons cornstarch

2 tablespoons baking soda

5 drops of your favorite essential oil scent

Combine all ingredients and mix well. Store in a lidded jar.

Body Powder

*This is a great gift when packaged in an antique salt
or seasoning shaker.*

16 tablespoons arrowroot or cornstarch or a blend of both

8 tablespoons baking soda

7 to 8 drops essential oil of your choice

Blend the cornstarch or arrowroot and baking soda and add enough essential oil to provide a pleasing scent. Store in a lidded container.

Foot Powder Deodorant

Your shoes will thank you.

2 ounces cornstarch

4 ounces unscented talcum powder

1 ounce baking soda

1 teaspoon powdered orrisroot

5 drops of your favorite scent

Combine all ingredients and mix well. Store in a lidded jar. (Use a large recycled spice jar with a perforated second lid so you can shake the powder into your shoes.)

Foot Spray

A gentle moisturizing spray for your feet.

¹/₂ cup vodka

¹/₄ cup witch hazel

¹/₂ teaspoon tea tree oil

15 drops sandalwood oil

Combine all ingredients and mix well. Store in a spray bottle. Always shake before using.

Honey Lip Balm

This will make 5 small pots of lip balm. Put them in the backpacks and gym bags of all your children.

1 cup almond oil

4 tablespoons beeswax

2 tablespoons honey

1 teaspoon essential oil, such as vanilla or rose

In a double boiler, melt the almond oil and beeswax. Remove from heat and immediately stir in the honey and essential oil. Pour into 2-ounce lidded containers. Let cool before covering.

The small plastic bottles in a travel kit are great to use for this balm.

Lemon Lip Balm

1 tablespoon petroleum jelly

1/2 teaspoon beeswax, grated

5 drops lemon oil

In a small microwave-proof bowl, heat the petroleum jelly and beeswax for 30 seconds on high until melted. Remove from oven. Stir in the lemon oil. Pour the mixture into a small screw-top jar or metal tin.

Peppermint Lip Balm

This tastes good and is good for your chapped lips.

1 tablespoon castor oil

1 tablespoon liquid glycerin

1 teaspoon liquid lanolin

8 drops peppermint oil

Blend all ingredients in a small bowl. Store in a small lidded pot.

Mouthwash

This mouthwash is as effective as commercial brands but doesn't taste like "medicine."

2 cups vinegar

2 tablespoons fresh chamomile

2 tablespoons fresh sage

2 tablespoons fresh comfrey

2 tablespoons fresh lavender

2 tablespoons fresh rosemary

In a medium nonreactive saucepan, bring the vinegar to a boil. Add all other ingredients. Immediately remove from heat and pour into a heat-resistant lidded jar. Let steep for 10 days. Strain through a coffee filter and pour into a screw-top jar. Use just like any other mouthwash.

CHAPTER SEVEN

Crafting with Clever Concoctions

Simple Ways to Make

Paint, Glue, Clay, Dough

and More

All-natural Coloring for Paints

These are alternative ways to create paints using a variety of food products and distilled water.

RED: Cut **beets** into small pieces and place in a saucepan. Cover with distilled water. Cook over medium heat for 30 minutes. Remove from heat and let cool. Strain juice into a glass jar.

YELLOW: Place **onionskins** in saucepan and cover with distilled water. Boil for 30 minutes. When cool, pour juice into glass jar.

GREEN: Place **spinach leaves** in saucepan and cover with distilled water. Boil 30 minutes. When cool, strain and pour into a jar.

BLUE: Place **blueberries** in a saucepan, cover with distilled water and boil 15 minutes. Cool and strain juice into a glass jar.

BROWN: Dissolve 1 teaspoon **instant coffee** in 2 tablespoons hot water. Let cool.

Mix the liquid dye with a paint medium (available in art and craft stores) to thicken. Use as you would any type of paint. The color is not permanent if not used within 2 to 3 days.

Body Paint

This type of nontoxic paint is ideal for Halloween or parties anytime. You can paint faces or create hand puppets. This is completely safe for even the most sensitive skin as long as the commercial cold cream you use is pure and unscented.

6 teaspoons cornstarch

3 teaspoons cold cream

3 teaspoons water

Food coloring

In the wells of a muffin tin, for each color mix 1 teaspoon cornstarch, $1/2$ teaspoon cold cream and $1/2$ teaspoon water. Blend thoroughly. Add a few drops of food coloring, stirring well to create the color of choice.

Bubble Paint

This is a great project to create an abstract work of art.
Each painting will be unique.

For each color:

2 teaspoons dishwashing liquid

3 tablespoons water

¼ cup powdered tempera

Blend the dishwashing liquid, water and powdered tempera in a lidded jar. To deepen the color, add more tempera. Set the jar on newspaper to protect the work surface. Gently blow the straw in the paint mixture. Absolutely do not suck in. The mixture tastes terrible and might make you sick. Keep blowing until the bubbles overflow. To create a bubble print, remove the jar and gently place a piece of paper on top of the overflow of bubbles. They will leave a print on the paper during and after the burst. Lay the paper flat to dry.

Doughy Paint

Kids love this dough that squeezes out of the bottle to create a three-dimensional paint. Have them spell their names on a board, and hang it in their rooms. Let them create art that is truly one of a kind.

1/4 cup flour

1/4 cup salt

1/4 cup water

2 tablespoons tempera paint color of choice

Mix all ingredients together until thoroughly blended. Pour into a plastic squeeze bottle such as a clean, recycled ketchup bottle.

Egg Tempera Paint

A simple paint to make on a rainy day.

I egg yolk (set aside egg white for later)

I teaspoon water

I teaspoon powdered tempera

Break up the egg yolk in a bowl. Measure 2 teaspoons and put in a jar. Add the water and blend. Gently add the powdered tempera and mix until smooth. Refrigerate and store in a lidded jar. (A baby food jar works perfectly.) The powdered tempera comes in a variety of colors. This paint will last for 1 to 2 months.

Paint a picture with the egg tempera paint and let dry. When finished, clean your brush. To accent the picture, brush on the egg white in any place you might like glitter to adhere. The egg white will act as a clear glue to hold the glitter, but it dries quickly so you need to apply glitter immediately then gently shake off excess.

Finger Paints

This is perfect to amuse the kids, and it is completely safe for youngsters who like to taste-test everything.

3 tablespoons sugar

1/2 cup cornstarch

2 cups cold water

Dish detergent

Food coloring

In a medium saucepan, mix the sugar and cornstarch together. Slowly stir in water and cook over medium heat, stirring constantly. Bring to a boil. The mixture will begin to thicken in about 5 minutes. Remove from heat and allow to cool completely. Pour 1/2 cup of the mixture into individual containers. To each, add a drop of detergent and food coloring, and mix to blend.

Store the paint in lidded wide-mouth jars, which are best for little hands.

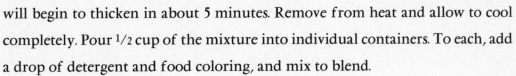

Milk Poster Paint

*This opaque paint is excellent for painting stage scenery, murals,
posters or waxed surfaces such as milk cartons. It is best to make only
the amount of paint you will need, although it can be kept overnight
in an airtight container. This paint is water-soluble.*

MAKES LESS THAN 1 CUP.

$1/4$ **cup powdered paint pigment**

$1/4$ **cup powdered milk**

2 teaspoons cornstarch

$1/2$ **cup warm water**

In a small bowl, mix the pigment, milk and cornstarch, then gradually add
the water, stirring until smooth and creamy.

Oil Paint Without Oil

This paint concoction is fabulous for your mini artist. The consistency is quite similar to oil paint. Because the colors blend together well, it's a great way to introduce color mixing to your children.

For each color:

1 tablespoon powdered tempera

1 tablespoon dishwashing soap

Mix the powdered tempera and dishwashing soap together until it is a smooth consistency. Store in small lidded glass containers, such as baby food jars.

Poster Paint

*This kind of paint is particularly good for making silkscreen
design, but it's versatile enough for any use. This paint is inexpensive
to make in large quantities.*

2 parts powdered pigment

I part liquid starch

Mix ingredients thoroughly. It should have a creamy consistency.

This paint adheres better than a water-based paint. Store in covered jars.

Watercolors

This is an inexpensive and good substitute for purchased watercolors.

1 tablespoon white vinegar

2 tablespoons baking soda

1 tablespoon cornstarch

¼ teaspoon glycerin

Food coloring

In a small bowl, mix the vinegar and baking soda. When the mixture stops bubbling, add the cornstarch and glycerin. Pour the mixture into an ice-cube tray. Stir in several drops of food coloring to each ice-cube square. The paint will be liquid at this point. Let it harden overnight.

Block Printing Ink

This form of printing goes back many years. To experience the original way of printing, try this.

3 tablespoons powdered pigment

1 tablespoon clear varnish

Mix the pigment and varnish thoroughly on a glass surface with a palette knife. Roll a brayer or roller* back and forth until the mixture has evenly coated the brayer/roller.

Roll the brayer over a carved wood or linoleum block. Press the block on the paper, and apply even weight. This same process is great for potato or rubber stamps.

*A wallpaper seam roller will work.

Invisible Ink

This is a mysterious ink to create a little mystery
in your letter writing.

Juice of 1 lemon

$1/2$ cup milk

1 tablespoon confectioners' sugar mixed with $1/4$ cup water

1 tablespoon baking powder mixed with $1/4$ cup water

1 tablespoon alum mixed with $1/4$ cup water

Blend all the ingredients and place in a lidded container.

Using a paintbrush or cotton swab, dip it in the mixture and write a message on a piece of white bond paper. Allow the ink to dry, and your message will be invisible. Place the message between two scraps of paper, and using a warm iron, gently apply heat. The message will reappear.

Transfer Ink

This transfer method works well with comic strips, images printed
from an ink jet color printer and copies made from a copy machine
(the ink must sit up on top of the paper and not be quickly absorbed).
Experiment to discover what kind of pictures transfer best. This
process can also be used on fabric.

MAKES APPROXIMATELY 3/4 CUP.

2 tablespoons soap powder, such as Ivory Snow

¹/₄ cup hot water

I tablespoon turpentine

Dissolve the soap powder in hot water and add the turpentine. Pour into a covered container for future use.

Brush the "ink" over the picture to be transferred. Wait about 10 seconds. Place a piece of paper over the picture and rub the paper with the back of a spoon. The picture will transfer to the paper.

Waterproof Ink

This ink is great for stenciling or painting on fabrics. Next time you send your kids to camp, label their clothes with this ink.

MAKES APPROXIMATELY 3/4 CUP.

1 tablespoon powdered clothes dye

2 teaspoons peppermint extract

1 tablespoon glycerin

3/4 cup distilled water

Combine the dye and the peppermint extract in a small bowl until dissolved. Blend in the glycerin. Add water while mixing thoroughly. Store in a bottle with a lid.

Pastel Crayons

These are big crayons for little hands.

1 ounce paraffin or candle wax

1 teaspoon linseed oil

3 tablespoons powdered paint pigment

In a double boiler, melt the wax over low heat. Remove from heat. Add the linseed oil and stir. Add the paint pigment and stir. Cover the end of an empty paper towel or toilet paper tube with waxed paper or aluminum foil. Secure the paper/foil with an elastic band. Pour a small portion of the mixture in the tube and let it harden. This will take about 1 to 2 hours. Pour the remaining mixture to fill the tube. Repeat this process to make additional colored crayons with different color pigments.

When the mixture hardens, the tube may be peeled away. Use as you would with any crayon. These are great fun for kids!

Hopscotch Sidewalk Chalk

This hard chalk will not work on chalkboards, but it's great on side-walks. And it actually will last longer than store-bought chalk. This is a great project and is fun to do . . . but beware, it is messy!

1 cup plaster of paris

¹/₂ cup cool water

Liquid tempera paint in various colors

Pour the plaster of paris into a disposable container such as a large clean margarine tub. Using a disposable stick (craft sticks are great), stir in most of the water. Add 2 or 3 tablespoons of liquid tempera, mixing well to remove any clumps. Add a little more water, mix and when it feels like you're mixing pancake batter, seal one end of an empty toilet or paper towel tube with waxed paper or foil secured tightly by an elastic band. Pour liquid into tube. Allow this to dry completely, about 24 hours.

Decoupage Paste

*Decoupage is the art of cutting out pieces of paper and mounting
them with a transparent paste to a hard surface.*

3 parts white household or school glue

1 part warm water

Mix the glue and water in a covered jar.

Cut out pictures from magazines to decoupage. Brush a thin layer of glue
on the back and front of all the pictures. (It may appear to have a white film,
but this will dry clear.) Apply pictures to hard surface. Let paste dry. Continue
to layer 3 to 4 coats of paste and let dry between applications. The more coats of
paste, the glossier the finish will be.

Flour-and-Water Paste

This classic paste is great for kids because the taste is terrible,
but it's nontoxic just in case the desire to eat glue kicks in.

³/₄ cup cold water

¹/₂ cup flour

3 cups water

In a large bowl, slowly pour the cold water into the flour, stirring constantly to make a paste. Next, boil the 3 cups of water in the microwave on high power for 3 minutes. Remove from oven and immediately pour paste into the boiling water, stirring constantly. Return to oven and microwave on medium for 2 minutes, or until the paste is thick and smooth. Store in a plastic squeeze container.

Thin Paste

This thin paste is great for scrapbooks, papier-mâché or collages.

MAKES APPROXIMATELY 1 PINT.

1/4 cup sugar

1/4 cup nonself-rising wheat flour

1/2 teaspoon powdered alum

1 3/4 cups water

1/4 teaspoon oil of cinnamon

In medium-size saucepan, mix together sugar, flour and alum. Gradually add 1 cup water, stirring vigorously to get rid of the lumps. Over medium heat, bring to a boil, and cook until clear and smooth, stirring constantly. Remove from heat and add remaining water and oil of cinnamon. Stir until mixed thoroughly.

Spread the paste with a brush or craft stick. Paste can be stored in a covered jar for several months.

Wallpaper Paste

*This paste spreads best when warm. It will keep for a few days
if you use the oil of cinnamon to prevent mold.*

MAKES APPROXIMATELY 1 1/2 GALLONS.

4 cups nonself-rising wheat flour

1 cup sugar

1 gallon warm water

1 quart cold water

1/2 teaspoon oil of cinnamon (optional)

Mix flour and sugar in a large saucepan. Over medium heat, slowly add
enough warm water to make a smooth paste. Then add the rest of the warm
water slowly, stirring vigorously to get rid of the lumps. Bring the mixture to a
boil, constantly stirring. Cook this mixture until it is thick and clear. Remove
from heat and dilute the mixture with cold water to desired consistency. Add
the oil of cinnamon if paste will not be used the same day it is made.

Seal and Envelope Gum

This glue is ideal for gluing paper to paper or to cardboard.
It is thicker than Stamp Gum (see page 159). This recipe makes
a lot so you can cover oodles of envelopes, labels or just
make big paper projects.

MAKES APPROXIMATELY 1/2 CUP.

6 tablespoons pure white vinegar

4 (1-ounce) packets unflavored gelatin

1 tablespoon lemon extract

In a small pan, bring the vinegar to a boil. Add the gelatin and stir until completely dissolved. Add the lemon extract and stir until well blended.

Spread the gum thinly on the back of a label or an envelope flap. Let dry. Moisten to apply.

Store in a covered jar. If the gum hardens, soften in a pan of warm water.

Stamp Gum

*Extend the life of stamps and stickers when the adhesive has
worn out with this simple homemade glue.*

1 packet (1/4-ounce) unflavored gelatin	3 tablespoons boiling water
	1/2 teaspoon white corn syrup
1 tablespoon cold water	1/2 teaspoon lemon extract

In a small bowl, pour the gelatin into the cold water. Set aside until it is softened. In a heat-proof bowl, combine the softened gelatin and boiling water and stir until completely dissolved. Add the remaining ingredients. Mix well. Pour into a small lidded glass jar.

This gum will gel overnight. To return it to a liquid state, warm container of gum in a pan of hot water.

Brush the gum thinly on to the back of a stamp or sticker. Apply it to the paper.

The mixture will keep for several months in a sealed container.

Halloween Light

It's easy to make ghost "figurines" for Halloween. Put a votive candle or light underneath and . . . Boo! (You can use this plaster of paris dipping cloth technique for other projects—let your imagination run wild at any time of the year.)

1½ parts plaster of paris

1 teaspoon powdered alum for each cup of water

1 part water

Cloth (gauze works best) or sheeting

In a large bowl, blend the plaster of paris and alum slowly into the water. Stir until creamy.

Dip cloth into the plaster mixture. Drape the cloth over a 2-liter bottle, wire, cardboard cone or anything that could serve as a base. You will have 15 to 20 minutes to mold the fabric before it dries. When it is hard, you can cut out eye and mouth holes.

Fixative

Commercial fixatives can be very expensive and quite toxic. This homemade version works as well, and you have more control than you would with those aerosol cans.

1 part pure white shellac

1 part denatured alcohol

Pour the shellac into a screw-top glass jar, add the alcohol and shake to combine. Pour the mixture into a spray bottle.

To fix chalk, charcoal, pencil or pastel drawings, apply fixative from a distance of about 20 inches with a light coating. Repeat two or three times, but do not soak the page.

Newspaper Clipping Preservative

This preservative will keep newspaper clippings from turning yellow.
Always remember to keep clippings out of direct sunlight.

MAKES APPROXIMATELY 1 QUART.

1 quart warm club soda

1 milk of magnesia tablet

Pour the club soda into a bowl. Drop the milk of magnesia tablet into the club soda and let it dissolve overnight. Stir mixture before using.

Carefully pour the preservative mixture onto a cookie sheet with high sides. Place the clippings in the liquid one layer at a time and let them get completely saturated. Carefully remove the clippings, and let them dry on a flat surface.

Bookbinding Glue

This glue is great for adhering cloth to cardboard, leather to leather or making notebook and scrapbook binders.

MAKES APPROXIMATELY $1/3$ CUP.

1 packet ($1/4$-ounce) unflavored gelatin

3 tablespoons boiling water

1 tablespoon vinegar

1 teaspoon glycerin

In a small heat-resistant dish, dissolve the gelatin in the boiling water. Add the remaining ingredients and stir.

While the glue is still warm, apply a thin layer with a brush.

Store glue in a covered jar. It will keep for several months. Over time it will gel. To use again, immerse jar in a pan of warm water to liquefy.

Glass Glue

This glue works well for glass-to-glass or wood-to-wood adhesion.
It is waterproof and is great for repairing china.

2 packets ($1/2$-ounce) unflavored gelatin

2 tablespoons cold water

3 tablespoons skim milk

Several drops oil of cloves (optional)

In a small heat-resistant bowl, pour the gelatin into the cold water and set aside. Heat the milk to a boiling point in the microwave and pour it into the gelatin until dissolved. Add the oil of cloves as a preservative, if you want to save the glue for more than one day.

While the glue is still warm, brush a thin layer on the item to be glued. Over time the glue will gel, which makes gluing odd-shaped objects easier to handle (i.e., marbles to cans).

Keep remaining glue in a covered jar. To return it to a liquid state, immerse in a pan of warm water.

Gooey Glue

This glue is child- and paper-friendly. The consistency makes it easy for kids to apply small amounts to small areas.

MAKES APPROXIMATELY 2 1/2 CUPS.

2 cups water

3 tablespoons cornstarch

4 tablespoons cold water

Microwave the water in a glass bowl on high for 3 minutes or until it comes to a boil. While microwaving, mix the cornstarch and cold water in a small bowl. Remove the boiling water from the oven and pour the paste into the water, stirring constantly. Return mixture to microwave on low power for 1 to 2 minutes to thicken. When liquid is clear and thick, remove from oven and let cool. Pour into a plastic squeeze container and label.

Milk Glue

This is a nontoxic glue to adhere paper to paper.

¹/₄ cup milk

1 teaspoon vinegar

Pinch of baking soda

Little water

In a small saucepan, slowly heat the milk over medium heat, stirring constantly. It should be hot but not boiling. Remove the milk from the stove and add the vinegar. A solid material will form in the milk. This is the protein which is called casein. Drain off the liquid from the solid material and rinse the casein in cool water. Squeeze out the water and put the casein in a cup. Add the pinch of baking soda and a little water and mix to make a smooth mixture about the consistency of yogurt.

Apply a thin layer to the back of paper for gluing.

Bread Dough Clay

This clay is ideal for making beads or small pieces of jewelry.

MAKES ENOUGH CLAY FOR A FEW BEADS.

I slice white bread

I teaspoon white glue

I tablespoon water

Food coloring

Clear glaze or clear nail polish

Cut the crust off the bread. Mix the glue and water and drop it onto the center of the bread. Knead the "dough" until it doesn't stick to your fingers. Divide the dough into several small piles and add a few drops of food coloring to each. Knead to blend in color.

The clay will begin to dry quickly on the outside, so make holes through the beads, if you wish, before it starts to harden. The clay will dry completely overnight. To preserve, spray with a clear glaze or paint with clear nail polish.

Ornament Clay

1/4 cup cold water

1/2 cup cornstarch

1/2 cup salt

1/2 cup water

In a small bowl, combine cold water and cornstarch. Set aside. In a small saucepan, bring to a boil the salt and 1/2 cup water. Gradually add the cornstarch mixture to the boiling water, and stir to break up the lumps. Stirring constantly, cook until the mixture is stiff like cookie dough. Remove from the heat. As soon as the mixture is cool enough to work with, turn out onto clean surface and smooth out with a rolling pin to 1/4-inch thickness.

The clay has a sandy texture. Once rolled out, you can cut it into shapes with cookie cutters. Don't forget to make a hole for hanging with a straw or skewer while moist. The clay will harden in 24 to 48 hours. When dry, the ornaments can be painted with water-based acrylic paint. To speed up drying, place on a cookie sheet in a 200-degree F oven for 1 hour.

Salt and Flour Clay

This clay can be used to make hand-rolled beads, cut-out
ornaments or molded shapes.

MAKES APPROXIMATELY 1¹/₂ CUPS.

³/₄ cup salt

³/₄ cup nonself-rising flour

2 teaspoons powdered alum

³/₄ cup water

2 tablespoons vegetable oil

Food coloring

Mix the salt, ¹/₂ cup of the flour and alum in a medium saucepan. Add water slowly, stirring to avoid lumps. Cook over low heat, and stir constantly. The texture will become rubbery, hard to stir and sticky. Remove from heat, and stir in the vegetable oil. Pour the mixture onto a plate or aluminum foil. Divide the mixture into as many portions as you would like to have colors. Add different food coloring to each portion. Knead each portion until the color is blended. If the clay is too sticky to handle well, add flour a bit at a time as you knead.

Sawdust Clay

Pieces made with this kind of "clay" will have a wood-grain appearance.

MAKES APPROXIMATELY 1 CUP.

1 cup sawdust

5 drops of food coloring (optional)

1 cup Thin Paste (see page 156)

Shellac or clear varnish (optional)

To color the clay, shake the sawdust and the food coloring in a glass jar. Spread on double sheets of newspaper to dry before mixing with the remaining ingredients. In a large bowl, mix sawdust and paste to thick dough-like consistency, turn out onto a flat surface and knead thoroughly. The amount of paste depends on the kind of sawdust used. The finer the sawdust, the smaller amount of paste will be needed before dough-like consistency is achieved.

Shape as with any clay. It will air dry in 2 to 3 days. To speed up drying, bake at 200 degrees F for 1 to 2 hours, depending on the size of the sculpture. To preserve the piece, spray with a shellac or varnish.

Soapsuds Clay

This clay dries to a very hard finish. It's ideal for simulating snow on your windowsill or Christmas tree branches.

MAKES APPROXIMATELY 1 CUP.

1 ½ cups soap powder, such as Ivory Snow

1 tablespoon warm water

In a large bowl, mix the soap powder and water with the electric mixer to a cake-icing consistency.

Apply the clay to any surface just as you would cake icing.

Coffee Dough

This dough will have a natural look to it when it dries.
The brown color and coffee-grind speckles will make your artwork
look as if it is made from stone.

1 cup flour

$^1/_2$ cup salt

1 cup used coffee grinds

$^1/_2$ cup cold leftover coffee

Blend all the ingredients in a bowl thoroughly. Put the dough on a floured surface. Knead it until smooth. The dough can be stored in an airtight container or plastic bag for 5 to 6 days.

Cooked Flour Dough

Use this dough to make cookie-cutter or handmade shapes.

2 cups flour

1 cup salt

2 cups water

2 tablespoons oil

1 tablespoon cream of tartar

In a large saucepan, blend all ingredients. Stirring constantly, cook the mixture over low heat until it looks like mashed potatoes. Remove the saucepan from heat and cool until ready to handle. Put the dough glob on a floured surface and knead until you have smooth dough. Roll the dough out with a rolling pin to desired thickness and use cutters to make ornaments or decorations, or shape by hand. It will harden in 2 to 3 days.

Crêpe Paper Dough

Crêpe paper dough is a concoction that likes to cling together, almost like a wet cloth. It can be easily draped over different forms, such as plastic bowls, tin cans or glasses. The dough color will be slightly lighter than the original crêpe paper. This dough dries hard and can be decorated and sealed with spray shellac.

I roll of crêpe paper

Water

1/2 cup flour

1/4 cup salt

Tear the crêpe paper into small pieces and soak in a large bowl of water for several hours. Drain and squeeze most of the water from the pulp. Measure 1 packed cup crêpe paper pulp into the mixing bowl. Add the flour and salt and press the mixture into a firm blob. Knead until it feels like workable dough. Store in an airtight lidded container until ready to use.

Modeling Dough

MAKES APPROXIMATELY 4 CUPS.

1 cup salt

1 1/2 cups hot water

4 cups flour

In a large bowl, mix the salt and hot water until the salt is dissolved. Slowly add the flour until thoroughly mixed. Turn the mixture out onto a hard surface and knead until soft. Place in covered container for several hours before using.

Shape dough into any object, or roll out and cut with a cookie cutter. Make sure the objects are not any thicker than 1 1/2 inches. Bake the objects on a cookie sheet for 1 hour at 300 degrees F. Let cool, then paint with watercolors or tempera. These objects can be preserved with a clear varnish or plastic fixative spray. Extra dough will keep for a week or more in an airtight container.

Dough to Play With

This homemade version of commercial dough is easy to make and completely nontoxic.

MAKES APPROXIMATELY 3 CUPS.

2¼ cups nonself-rising wheat flour

1 cup salt

1 tablespoon powdered alum

4 tablespoons vegetable oil

1½ cups boiling water

Food coloring or poster paints

In a large bowl, combine the flour, salt and alum, then stir in the vegetable oil until blended. Pour in the boiling water, and stir until it holds together. Remove the dough to a flat, clean surface, and knead until smooth. Divide the dough into several clumps. Add a few drops of food coloring or poster paint to each clump. Knead until the color is evenly distributed. Shape as desired. Pieces will dry completely in 2 to 3 days.

Store unused dough in an airtight container. It will keep for 4 to 6 weeks.

Sand and Cornstarch Modeling Dough

This is a very grainy dough that can be dried naturally if you don't want the bother of turning on the oven.

MAKES APPROXIMATELY 2 CUPS.

1 cup sand

1/2 cup cornstarch

1 teaspoon powdered alum

3/4 cup hot water

Food coloring (optional)

In a saucepan, mix the sand, cornstarch and alum. Add the water and mix well. Add food coloring if desired. Cook over medium heat until thick, stirring constantly. Allow to cool.

Mold, and dry the objects in the sunshine. To enhance your work of art, paint with acrylic paints. Store leftover dough in an airtight container.

Tea Dough

This dough, like its coffee cousin, also simulates a natural stone appearance. It works well to make tiny beads for jewelry.

4 tablespoons flour

I tablespoon salt

I tablespoon water, or tea for extra color

2 tablespoons used tea leaves

Mix the flour, salt and water in a bowl. Add the tea leaves until the dough begins to fall apart. In your hands, shape dough into a ball. Place the ball on a clean surface, and knead it until smooth. Divide to make beads, and be sure to insert holes in the beads before they begin to harden. Store leftover dough in an airtight container.

Papier-Mâché

This is the classic way to make puppets, masks,
bowls or small sculptures.

Newspaper

Thin Paste (see page 156)

Tear newspaper into strips. For large objects, tear 1 to 1 1/2 inch-wide strips, and for smaller objects, tear thinner strips. If paste is too thick, thin with water. Brush the strips with the paste or dip the strips in the paste, drawing off excess paste.

Layer the glued strips of newspaper over a base (i.e., balloon, lightbulb, plastic bowl or jar depending on the final shape you want) first in one direction and then in a second layer in the opposite direction. Continue layering until you have at least 4 or 5 layers. Larger objects should have more layers so they are sturdy. It will take about 1 to 2 days to dry. The object can be decorated or painted.

Papier-Mâché Pulp

This mixture can be used like modeling clay.

Newspaper

2 quarts warm water

1/2 cup thick paste (use recipe for

    Thin Paste, but only use 1 cup

    of water, see page 156)

Oil of cloves

Poster paints

Shellac

Tear a newspaper into approximately 50, 1 by 10-inch strips. Pour the warm water into a large plastic dishpan. Sprinkle the strips in the pan, and completely submerge them under the water. Set aside overnight. With an electric mixer, beat soaked paper until you have a smooth pulp. Strain off excess water and squeeze pulp with your hands until nearly dry. In a large bowl gradually add the paste to the pulp/and mix to a soft clay consistency with an electric mixer. Add a few drops of oil of cloves to prevent mold from forming.

Shape or model as with clay. Place the finished object in a spot where the air can circulate around it until it is completely dry. Allow 4 to 6 days to dry. If the object cracks while drying, mend it with additional pulp. Paint the object with poster paints and then shellac.

Funny Putty

What a terrific inexpensive treat for kids. Package the putty
in plastic Easter eggs as party favors.

Food coloring

¹/₂ cup Elmer's glue (use *only* this brand)

¹/₂ cup liquid starch

In a bowl, mix food coloring into Elmer's glue. Slowly add starch to colored glue. Knead the mixture until it comes to the right texture—like putty! Store in a tightly covered container. The putty will begin to harden if left in the open air for more than a couple of hours.

Salt Map Mixture

This mixture is for making three-dimensional maps or dioramas.

1 part salt

1 part nonself-rising wheat flour

2/3 part water

Food coloring or poster paints

Mix salt and flour. Add water to get the consistency of thick icing. The more water you use, the longer the mixture will take to dry. Add food coloring before molding, or mold and paint when dry. Using a piece of wood or heavy cardboard as a base, spread the mixture out and shape it to make any landscape you want.

Colored Sand or Rice

Have you ever been to a fair or theme park where you pay $3 or $4 to have your child pour layers of colored sand into a bottle? Well, this is how they do it. Colored sand is attractive to use in clear, glass containers for decoration or any kind of sand art craft project.

½ cup clean, sifted sand or uncooked rice

¼ cup alcohol

Food coloring

To clean the sand, use a sieve to sift the fine grains of sand into a bucket. Cover the sand with clean water. Drain the sand carefully through the sieve. Repeat this until the water runs clear. (For rice, cleaning is not necessary.) Pour the clean sand or rice into a jar. Add the alcohol and food coloring. Stir the mixture or screw on the lid and shake vigorously to distribute color evenly. Let the sand sit in the colored alcohol for at least 20 minutes (about 5 to 6 minutes for rice). Then, carefully pour out the extra alcohol using the sieve. Spread the sand out to dry on newspaper. Stir it around several times, so that it will dry thoroughly. When it is completely dry, pour it back into the lidded jar. Repeat this step several times for various colors.

Decorative Eggshells

This will make beautiful eggs to use in decorative bowls or to hang as ornaments. The eggs are quite fragile, so be careful.

6 white eggs

Lacy patterns: parsley, doilies, bits of lace

Used panty hose

Rubber bands

Outer skins from 4 to 5 yellow onions*

4 cups water

*Use some of the other ingredients described in "All-Natural Coloring for Paints" (see page 138) to vary the colors.

Blow each egg out of its shell by gently twisting a poultry skewer or sharp awl into the larger end of the egg, through the shell and into the yolk. Turn the egg upside down over a bowl and carefully bore another, smaller hole in the smaller end of the egg. Gently blow into the smaller hole until all the egg is in the bowl. Wash the eggshell and allow to dry. Arrange bits of lacy leaves, lace or doily designs around each eggshell and wrap the egg and designs in a piece of panty hose. Secure the panty hose snugly around the egg with a rubber band. Arrange the eggshells in a microwave-safe glass bowl with the onionskins and cover with 4 cups of water. Cook in the microwave on high power for 3 minutes then simmer on medium power for 5 minutes. Remove the bowl from the oven and drain the water. Allow the shells to cool in the bowl before unwrapping.

Flower preservative

*You will be able to have a fresh flower bouquet
that lasts forever anytime.*

Fresh flowers (roses, pansies, daisies, mums, sweet peas)

Floral wire

Airtight container

Plastic bag

Borax

Soft brush

Remove the natural stems from the blooms, and replace them with the wire by running it through the throat of the flower and twisting it. Line the container with the plastic bag. Pour the borax into the plastic bag to cover the bottom about 1 inch. Place the flower blossom facedown in the borax and add as many flowers as the container can hold without crowding. Pour another layer of borax until the flowers are covered. Twist the plastic bag closed as tightly as possible. Close the container, and let the flowers sit for at least 5 weeks. Remove the flowers, and carefully brush away the borax.

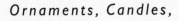

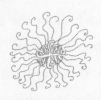

CHAPTER EIGHT

Gift Recipes You Can't Eat

Ornaments, Candles,

Paper Products

and Treats for the Pets

Apple-Cinnamon Ornaments

*These beautiful ornaments have the unexpected bonus of
giving off a heavenly apple scent for many weeks.*

1 1/2 **cups ground cinnamon**

1 **cup applesauce**

1/4 **cup white school glue**

Preheat oven to 200 degrees F. Thoroughly mix the cinnamon, applesauce and glue in a bowl. The "dough" should have the consistency of cookie dough. Remove from the bowl and knead. Place it back in the bowl, cover with plastic wrap and let it sit for at least 30 minutes. Remove the dough; knead again until it is smooth. Roll out the dough between two pieces of waxed paper until it is 1/8 to 1/4-inch thick. (The thicker ones keep their shape better.) Cut out desired shapes with cookie cutters. Use a straw to punch a hole in the top for hanging. Gently place the shapes on a nonstick cookie sheet and cook in the oven for 1 1/2 to 2 hours. Turn them over every half hour until they are hard. Don't let them burn. Remove from oven and cool on a rack. Run a decorative piece of ribbon or yarn through the hole to hang ornaments.

Barbecue Brush

This is a perfect accompaniment as a gift with a bottle
of homemade barbecue sauce.

Sprigs of parsley, sage, rosemary and thyme

Gently yet securely, tie the herb sprigs to the handle of a wood spoon with twine. Be sure to have about a 4-inch length of herbs standing above the handle of the spoon.

Use the bowl of the spoon to pour the sauce on the meat, and brush it on with the herbs.

Bird Cookies

Treat the birds to some homemade treats.

1³/₄ pounds suet

¹/₂ cup sunflower seeds

¹/₂ cup crushed peanuts

¹/₂ cup cracked corn kernels

Melt the suet in a pan over medium-low heat. Stir in the sunflower seeds, peanuts and cracked corn kernels. Spoon mixture into plastic candy molds. Don't forget to poke a hole in the top with a drinking straw. Let dry and pop out of the molds. String a decorative ribbon through the top, and hang in the trees for the birds.

Bird Crackers

Do you ever wonder what to give neighbors for Christmas?
You want to remember them, but the family budget does not allow
for a whole lot. Just make a few bird crackers and package
in pretty cello bags.

Peanut butter

12 saltine crackers

Birdseed

Spread peanut butter on both sides of the crackers and dip in the birdseed, completely covering the cracker with birdseed. Let sit for about 15 minutes. The cracker will soften a little, and you can easily punch a hole in the top to string a ribbon through.

Doggie Treats

Even pets can enjoy something homemade.

1 1/2 cups whole-wheat flour

2 teaspoons brown sugar

1 teaspoon garlic powder

1/2 teaspoon onion powder

1/2 cup powdered dry milk

1 teaspoon beef bouillon

1/2 teaspoon salt

6 tablespoons meat drippings

1 egg, beaten

1/2 cup ice water

Preheat oven to 350 degrees F. Mix together all ingredients except the meat drippings, egg and water. Cut in the drippings until mixture resembles corn-meal. Mix in the egg. Add just enough water to make the mixture form a ball. Roll to about 1/2-inch thickness and cut into shapes by hand or using a dog bone cookie cutter. Bake on a greased cookie sheet for 30 minutes. Cool and serve.

Fruit Baskets for the Birds

This is an inexpensive and easy-to-make bird feeder. Nothing will be wasted since both you and the birds can enjoy this treat.

Oranges and grapefruits

Jute

Birdseed

Cut the fruit in half, eat the fruit or make juice and save the rind. Let the rinds dry in the sun for a day. Poke two holes in the sides of the fruit with the ice pick. Put jute through the holes and knot on the outside. Fill with birdseed and hang from your trees. The birds will love you!

Charcoal Crystals

Not only will your kids be delighted with this experiment
in creating "crystals," you'll amaze dinner guests if you use this
as a centerpiece.

Several charcoal briquettes

5 tablespoons salt

5 tablespoons bluing

5 tablespoons water

1 tablespoon ammonia

Food coloring

Place the briquettes in the bottom of a shallow glass dish or fish bowl. In a separate bowl, combine the salt, bluing, water and ammonia and mix. Pour the mixture over the briquettes. Drop a few drops of food coloring over the mixture, and crystals will begin to form. They will continue to grow and be colorful for several days.

Cinnamon Cones

*These are beautiful decorations for the hearth during the holiday
season. The cones also make great fire starters. The scent lingers
for 3 to 4 weeks. If you are going to give them
as gifts, package them in a plastic bag to keep the oil from evaporating.*

8 pounds white spruce cones

2 pounds large cinnamon chips

1 pound 1-inch cinnamon sticks

1 pound 3-inch cinnamon sticks

2 ounces cinnamon oil

In a large plastic garbage bag, mix cones and cinnamon chips and sticks.
Drop the oil a little at a time, then toss cones in the bag. Repeat the process until
all the oil is used. Leave the cones sealed in the bag for 6 weeks, tossing occasionally to redistribute the oil.

Crayon Crunch Craft Paper

This makes colorful paper for the kids to use to wrap presents or a work of art that you can proudly hang on the refrigerator door. Excess crayon that is not absorbed may crack on the paper but will leave a color impression that will add to the overall effect of the work.

16-by-16-inch sheet of white or light-colored craft paper

Bits and pieces of broken crayons, paper wrapping removed

Fold the craft paper into quarters score folds and unfold. Lay the paper out on a surface protected by newspapers. Using a vegetable peeler, shave different colors of crayon onto the surface of the craft paper until it is fairly evenly covered. (Because using a vegetable peeler is often a challenge for youngsters, you may want to make piles of shavings of different-colored crayons on a separate sheet of newspaper and let the kids sprinkle the shavings on the craft paper by hand.)

Place several layers of paper towel on the floor of the microwave. Lay the crayon-covered craft paper on top of the paper towel. (It will probably not lie that, but that won't affect the end result.) Microwave on medium to high power for 5 to 10 minutes or until the shavings begin to melt.

To protect small hands, make sure your young artists are wearing oven mitts or old winter gloves for this next step. Carefully remove the paper from the oven and lay it on a flat surface protected by newspaper. Refold in half or into quarters, and press all over the paper by hand to mush the melted crayon into pretty abstract designs. Unfold the paper immediately and let it cool.

Fragrant Finger Towels

After a dinner party, pass a tray of these around to
the delight of your guests.

Pretty colorful washcloths

Sprigs of scented geranium, lavender and lemon verbena

Rinse and wring out the washcloths. Fold the washcloths in half, and place several sprigs of the herbs on the cloth. Fold again and roll up. Place the rolls on a plate, place in the microwave and heat for 1 1/2 minutes on high.

Let your guests pick a towel and empty the herbs onto the plate. Serve with tongs, if the towels are very hot.

Crêpe Paper Raffia

*This is an inexpensive way to create sturdy and colorful cord
that is ideal for use on gift packages and baskets.*

Strips of crêpe paper (2 to 3 inches wide)

Thread one end of the crêpe paper through the hole of an empty thread spool. Twist and pull the entire length of crêpe paper through the spool. This simple action twists the crêpe paper to form a strong, decorative cord.

Flower Candle

This project lets you enjoy pressed flowers and leaves
throughout the whole year.

1¹/₂- to 2-inch diameter white candle about 6-inches high

Selection of pressed flowers or small leaves

Small cube of paraffin

Fill the can of a double boiler with enough hot water to reach the shoulder of the candle when it is immersed. Holding the candle by the wick, immerse in the hot water for about 45 seconds. Remove the candle, and working quickly, press a few flowers and leaves onto the softened wax around the lower part of the candle. Refill the can with very hot water and re-dip the candle again briefly to soften the wax surface and seal in the pressed flowers or leaves. In a microwave on medium heat for 3 to 4 minutes, melt a bowl of paraffin. Using a small paintbrush, coat the flowers with a thin layer of wax.

Herb Candles

These attractive and inexpensive herb-scented candles have a unique texture and a gorgeous scent.

Old candles

Ground herbs

3- to 4-inch diameter candle

Melt like-colored old candles in double boiler. Spread the ground herbs onto a flat, clean surface close to the stove. Holding the wick of the whole candle, dip it into the melted wax. Immediately roll it in the ground herbs. The herbs will adhere easily to the hot wax. Then dip the candle again into the melted wax just to cover the herbs but leaving the bumpy texture. Set the candle aside and let it harden.

Juice Can Candles

2 pounds household paraffin

20 drops apple essential oil (or any flavor you might like)

2 empty, clean frozen orange juice containers

2 (5-inch) emergency candles

Melt the paraffin in a double boiler over low heat. Once the paraffin is totally melted, add the apple essential oil and stir. Carefully pour the melted paraffin into the clean juice cans, filling them about 2/3 full. Let this set up for just a few minutes. Place one of the emergency candles in the middle of each can. At this point, it should stick to the bottom. If you put the candle in too soon, it, too, will begin to melt and sink into the can. This is why you must wait for the wax to become lukewarm. Let set for about 45 minutes. Reheat the remaining paraffin and cap off the top of the candle in the juice can. Make sure the wax does not cover up the top of the candle. Let sit overnight. (After about an hour, you could even put it in the refrigerator.) The next morning, cut the can above the candle and peel it away. (I like to use these cans because they are usually slick inside, and the cardboard sides slit easily.)

Recycled Candles

You can use almost any size or shape container to create distinctive candles with recycled wax. Try flowerpots (glass, pottery or clay), wineglasses, sugar bowls, creamers, vases, jars or anything that will hold wax. Glass vessels are the best containers to use.

Old candles

Birthday candles

Soup or coffee can

Vegetable oil spray

4 to 5 drops essential oil (if the candles you melt are unscented)

In a 250 degree F oven, preheat the container mold for about 10 minutes. (The wax will pour more evenly.) Gather old leftover candles (drippy, broken, bad colors). Melt like colors in a double boiler over medium to low heat. Using tongs carefully remove the wicks once the wax has melted. Remove the preheated container from the oven. Pour enough wax to come within a $1/8$ inch of the top. Let the wax start to harden 3 to 5 minutes, then stick a birthday candle in the middle of the wax, leaving the wick of the birthday candle visible by at least $1/8$ inch. Let all this harden for several hours. Melt more wax, and top the candle off to fill the container to the top, but be sure to not cover the birthday candle completely.

Marbleized Paper

*Create unique stationery, note cards, bookmarks or papers
to cover containers. You're only limited by your own creativity—and
no two pieces will be alike!*

Artist's oil paint

1 teaspoon paint thinner

Water

Squirt a little glob of paint into a paper cup. Add the paint thinner and mix thoroughly until the consistency is that of milk. Pour about 2 inches of water in a 4-inch deep aluminum pan slightly larger than the piece of paper you'll be using. With a paintbrush, dribble small drops of paint onto the surface of the water. Repeat with several colors on the same water. Float a piece of paper on the surface of the water for 8 to 10 seconds. The paper will pick up the floating paint and create a marbleized look. Carefully lift the paper off the surface of the water and lay it, paint side up, on a flat surface protected by several layers of newspaper to dry.

Permanent Sand Castles

Kids will love this when they can't get to the beach. Make sure the "sand dough" is cooled enough for little hands.

2 cups sand

I cup cornstarch

I cup water

Blend the sand, cornstarch and water in an old saucepan. Cook over low heat, stirring continuously, until the mixture begins to thicken. Remove from heat and let it cool. Place the blob on a heavy piece of cardboard or wood (so you can transport the finished object and to protect the countertop or table). Mold into a castle or any simple shape you like.

Petal Cubes

This simple touch adds a lot to any liquid served.

Dried and pressed rose petals*

* To dry and press rose petals, lay the petals in a single layer between two paper towels. Place them in the middle of a large book (telephone book, encyclopedia) for two weeks. Replace the paper towels with clean ones, and leave in the book another two weeks. Remove and use in a variety of projects.

Fill an ice-cube tray halfway with water and freeze. Place a rose petal on each cube and fill with water. Freeze the ice tray until ready to use.

Pinecone Flames

A beautiful fire can only be enhanced by these pinecone flame starters. Always use rubber gloves when mixing acidic ingredients.

1 1/2 **gallons hot water**

1/2 **pound copper sulfate (green flame)**

1/2 **pound boric acid (red flame)**

1/2 **pound calcium chloride (orange flame)**

Bushel of pinecones

Pour 1/2 gallon of the water and one chemical into each of three plastic containers. Stir until all the chemicals are dissolved. Divide cones into three batches. Immerse the pinecones in one of the three liquids and soak for 24 hours. Remove pinecones and let them dry in the sun for 48 hours. They must be completely dry, or they won't burn.

Scented Drawer Liners

Create your own unique scented drawer liners with this simple project.

Wallpaper or wrapping paper (any kind of paper but avoid shiny, wipe-clean or steam-resistant surfaces as the paper needs to be porous to absorb the scent)

Cotton balls

Essential oil of your choice

2 ounces crushed rose petals

1 ounce lavender

elastic bands

large plastic bag

Cut the paper to fit your drawers or shelves. Moisten a cotton ball with the essential oil. Rub the cotton ball on the underside of the paper. Sprinkle the rose petals and lavender thickly on the pattern side of the paper. Repeat, layering each piece of treated paper. Roll them up, secure the roll with elastic bands, and seal them in a plastic bag. Leave them for 4 weeks.

Remove the liners from the plastic bag, brush away all the rose petals and lavender (save this to make great sachets) and line your drawers.

Scented Stationery

Make your letters memorable with a beautiful
scent to match your sentiments.

Corrugated cardboard

Box of stationery of your choice

Essential oil

Pretty cotton fabric

Cut a piece of corrugated cardboard to fit the bottom of the box of sta-tionery. Generously pour drops of essential oil on the rippled side of the card-board. Cover with the fabric. Place the cardboard in the bottom of the box of stationery with the rippled side of the cardboard up. Replace the stationery in the box and close. (The fabric covering on the cardboard keeps the stationery from becoming stained from the oil.) Keep the box closed for about a week. When not in use, keep the box closed, as the oils will evaporate too quickly. This makes a wonderful gift, and, for an added touch, enclose a bottle of the essen-tial oil with more ideas for additional uses.

Snow Globe Mixture

Use old thrift-shop or flea-market figurines to
create a unique snow globe.

Clear-drying epoxy

Small plastic or ceramic figurine

Glass jar with screw-on lid

Distilled water

Pinch of glitter

$1/2$ teaspoon glycerin

Glue a figurine onto the lid of a glass jar. Set aside. Fill the jar to the top with the distilled water. Add the glitter and glycerin. Screw the lid on tightly. Shake whenever the mood strikes you.

Sugar Flowers

These little blossoms look wonderful as decorations for cakes, trays of food, place cards and the base of candles . . . the possibilities are endless. Some flowers are edible, but I tend to say no to eating flowers that are brushed with raw egg.

¹/₂ cup sugar

1 egg white

Freshly picked blossoms only—no stems (pansies, violets, rosebuds or petals)

In a blender or food processor, process the sugar until it is a fine powder. Pour sugar into a shallow bowl and set aside. In a separate bowl, beat the egg white until foamy. Paint each blossom with the egg white using a soft artist's brush, then sprinkle the blossom with the sugar powder, and carefully lay the blossom on waxed paper to dry. The flowers will dry in the positions you arrange them, so be careful to spread out the petals. Sprinkle with a bit more sugar and gently shake off any excess sugar. Dry the flowers in the microwave on medium power for 70 seconds, then on low for up to 3 minutes if the drying is not complete. Let stand to set. Carefully remove the completely dried flowers and layer them on tissue paper in a box. The flowers will keep for up to 6 to 7 months in a cool, dry place.

Porcelain Flowers

These types of flowers are very expensive to buy in the store.
This simple recipe will make it easy for you to create your
own porcelain arrangements.

6 to 8 plastic flowers

1 pint high-gloss white enamel paint

1 pint varnish

1/2 pint turpentine

Dust, wash and air-dry plastic flowers. In a large plastic dishpan, combine all the wet ingredients. Dip each flower into the glaze individually. Shake off excess glaze, and stand flowers in a soft-drink bottle to dry. This will take approximately 48 hours.

Arrange flowers into a beautiful, permanent bouquet.

Index